WRITING AND RELEASING RAPIDLY

INDIE INSPIRATION FOR SELF-PUBLISHERS, BOOK 1

ELANA M JOHNSON

WRITING AND RELEASING RAPIDLY

ABOUT ELANA M. JOHNSON

Hello! I'm Elana Johnson, a two-time USA Today bestselling author, Amazon bestselling author, Kindle All-Star Author, and have been making six-figures just with my writing since 2016. Three years, going on four with that income, and it goes UP each year not down.

I started writing in 2007, and I've been in the business through ups, downs, curves, pits, and more. I started in traditional publishing and have had 4 literary agents sell my work from here to France, in audio, paper, and ebook formats.

I've written for Hallmark. I've worked with editors from four publishing houses. I've had big deals and highs, and low lows and slumps.

Through it all, I kept writing.

I entered the self-publishing scene in 2014 as a "screw

it" way to tell my publisher they'd be upset they passed on my book. No lie. As if they cared. LOL.

But *I* cared, and I wanted to write what I wanted to write.

Go back and read that line again. In today's marketplace, it's all about writing to market. I do that...and I don't. I write what *I* want to write. This was a lesson I learned in 2013, when Simon & Schuster wanted a book similar to the young adult dystopian trilogy I'd already sold to them. So I gave them that. And they passed on it because...it was TOO similar to the YA dystopian trilogy I'd already sold to them.

I was like, SCREW IT. Some of you might use more colorful language.

But that defining moment in my career turned me to self-publishing, and I now only write what I want to write.

You don't have to write military sci-fi just because it's popular. Or billionaire romance. Or erotica. I know a lot of authors, and every one of them gets tired of writing what they're writing. The reason we keep doing it?

We love it.

If you don't, it'll show in your books and eventually you'll burn out. And since the point of this book is to help you write and produce and publish FASTER, we don't want you burning out or being discouraged in the process.

But I think that's first. Write what you love.

So when I published in 2014, I published a YA contemporary romance novel in verse. Say that five times fast. ;)

It was a book of my heart. It went to four acquisitions meetings at traditional houses and no one would buy it. "Verse novels aren't in," they'd say. Or "we don't know how to position this in the market," I heard.

So I self-published it, and I still freaking love that book. It doesn't sell anything. It did at first, but our Indie Publishing Climate (IPC) doesn't support books just taking off on their own like the self-publishing boom of late 2011 and early 2012. Yes, I was around then too.

Today's IPC is different, with so many more players in the game. But that's not what this book is about. This book is about rapid releasing and why you might choose this method to launch a series, or your career.

I've sidetracked again. I do that a lot. Sorry.

Back to 2014. The self-published novel did okay. I wrote another novel-in-verse and published it too. I had some old YA SFF on my hard drive, and I published that too. I remember a distinct feeling I had when I put that first book up on KDP (Kindle Direct Publishing).

It was addicting.

I wanted to do it more.

I *needed* to do it more.

And I did a lot of it wrong. But I had my traditionally published YA dystopian novels, some YA SFF out there, an adult fantasy that Amazon Press picked up, and things were going okay. Not great. Just okay.

I hit a major slump and flailed around for about 18

months. I was still writing, sure, but my books weren't selling, and I honestly wondered what the point was.

Some of you might be in that boat right now. Or the ship you used to be in is sinking, and you're wondering if you get in the lifeboat or abandon writing, er, the ship altogether.

I've been there.

If you haven't been there as an author yet, you simply haven't been around long enough. Or you're really lucky. LOL. Or maybe both.

The point is, we've all been there.

For me, I liken it to being a pilot. I'm in the plane, and things are going okay. Then there's a bird strike, and I have a choice to make. Water landing in the Hudson in January? Or death?

Both of those options are bad, right? Captain Sullenberger knows. Watch *Sully* and you'll know too.

But I can't think of that airplane pilot or watch that movie without sobbing. Because *I get it*. I've been in that seat, thinking *What the heck am I going to do now?*

Maybe I should just quit.

What's the point? No one reads my books.

I can't make money at this.

Etc, etc. etc.

If you're there, accept his virtual hug.

And don't give up.

It's time to get smart.

So let's get smart.

GETTING SMART

There are probably a dozen books about writing to market. I'm not going to reinvent the wheel, but I am going to start at the beginning.

You should too. Don't skip some steps in your publishing career the way I did. Or if you already have, one of the greatest things about Indie Publishing is you can fix those mistakes. (That back log of books on my hard drive I self-published? They're not for sale anymore. You're welcome.)

So up first, we need to talk teaching.

I'm a teacher by profession. I spent almost twenty years in an elementary classroom, teaching hundreds of students a day as they rotated in and out of my computer lab every thirty minutes. Just take a moment and imagine that.

It was my life. I was very good at it. I have a teacher's heart, and I want everyone to learn, do what they can do, and be successful.

That's why I'm writing this book. I want you to learn what you need to do to be successful. You may not be able to do everything in this book. You *can't* do what someone else does. You can only do what you can do.

I think that's so important that I'm going to type it again: *You can only do what you can do.*

And we can all learn. But we need to learn smartly.

In teaching, we sit in meetings for four or five days before the students come to school at the beginning of the year. Some meetings are good, and some are bad. I mean, they're meetings. But I learned something very early in my teaching career that applies to Indie Publishing: Start as you mean to go.

When you start a school year with children, you better do it in such a way that you can tolerate their subsequent behavior for the next 10 months of your life. If you don't... it's very hard to fix.

Indie Publishing is the same way. You should start as you mean to go. This includes decisions on:

Genre – what are you going to spend your time writing? Can that genre sustain you over many books and many years (hopefully) of your career? Do you like writing those types of books? And I mean, *really* like writing those types of books? Because you'll be writing a lot of them. Even the most seasoned authors get tired of writing the same books over and over. Or maybe that's just me. ;)

How saturated in this genre? Can you expand to other types of books within this genre? Or are you limited to young adult dystopian novels or zombie romance novels?

TIP: Think big, then niche down. For example, my pen name of Liz Isaacson writes Christian contemporary romance. That's BIG. But if you niche that down, she's one of the only authors writing Christian contemporary *western* romance. Not historical cowboys. Contemporary cowboys. Christian cowboys. Cowboy romances. That's much smaller.

Think big so you have a little bit of room to move around.

Niche down so you can dominate the category.

Here's another example. Elana Johnson (that's me too) writes clean contemporary romance. That's big. It includes YA and adult. It's clean/sweet. It's contemporary. But I can move within that however I want.

I niched down to beach romance, because I freaking love beach romances. But I can do oceans, rivers, or lakes. I can do islands. I can write billionaires. I can write football heroes. I can write princes. I have leeway all over the niche to write any kind of beach romance I want. But it's still beach romance, and I still love writing it.

So STOP AND THINK: What is your big genre? How have you niched down? And can you write this niche and big genre for many books and many years? If you don't know the answers to these questions or haven't thought about it, you haven't started as you mean to go. You've just started. It's a step, but it could be the wrong one, in the wrong direction.

You can fix it later, sure. Heaven knows I've made more than a few fixes in my career. But if you start as you mean to go, there's less work to do later.

Pricing – you train readers what to expect from you. This includes your decision to enroll your books in Kindle Unlimited (exclusive distribution from Amazon only) or not. Start as you mean to go. 99¢ readers will buy 99¢ books. They might not buy something priced higher than that. What are you willing to price your books at? Where does that path take you?

Name – do you need a pen name? Why or why wouldn't you do one? Initial or no initial? Do a search on Amazon and see what names are already being used that you're thinking of using.

I did a pen name and Liz was born in 2015 because at that time, I was still heavily entrenched in the YA SFF market. Christian cowboys didn't fit with that.

Since then, Elana has been up and down and around, and completely rebranded. Told you I've made some mistakes and attempted to fix them. You can too. If you're reading this and going, "Oh, crap..." all is not lost.

You just have work to do.

And hopefully, it's *smarter* work than you did last time.

And lastly, but I think the biggest one, is goals. What are your goals with your Indie publishing? This can be anything to "I want to make money," to "I want to pay off my mortgage," to "I want to make enough to quit my job."

Those are all monetary goals. Money goals. You want to make money with your writing. That's a great goal, but I find that many people have not defined it well enough.

In teaching, we have concrete goals we examine every week. "By the midyear assessment, 80% of fourth graders will reach mastery on their times tables through twelve."

It's defined. It's specific. It's tied to a timeline. It's attainable. We actually call them SMART goals.

S – specific

M – measurable

A – attainable

R – realistic (in small business, you'll see the term relevant here)

T – time-bound

What's your SMART goal for your publishing? Is it defined at all? Is it specific? How much time have you given yourself to achieve it? Is it attainable? I have a lot of thoughts on goals I'll save for another time.

Fine, I'll just say one: I think it's okay to "dream big" too, and everyone should have an "outrageous goal" they want to hit. For me, this year in 2019, mine is to make a half a million dollars by selling books. Can I do it? I don't know. But it's defined. It's specific. It's tied to the year. I've broken it down into steps to make it *appear* attainable. I know what I need to do to achieve it.

Do you know WHAT you need to do to achieve your goal?

If not, how in the world will you do it?

Teachers don't teach like that. We know the goal. We know where kids need to be at benchmarks (in-between) times in order to meet the goal. We know what to do with the children who've already met the goal, and we know how to provide extra support to those struggling to meet the in-between benchmark goals leading up to the Big Goal.

Authors shouldn't write, publish, or market without knowing the goal.

Do you know any of those things for your publishing goals?

If not, STOP AND THINK. Right now. Get a piece of paper out or open a new email to yourself or whatever.

What are your goals for your writing and publishing? Define them. Be specific. Tie them to a timeframe. Are they attainable?

What steps can you outline that will help you reach that goal?

For me, I broke it down into income per month, and then per day. I know how much I need to make every month and every day of that specific month (because they each have a different number of days...) to make the $500,000 I want to make.

And if I don't make it, what intervention methods will I implement? Sales? Free days? Boxed sets? I have plans for those too, should I need them.

I have the goal. I have a plan if I'm not meeting the goal.

And my plan if I'm exceeding the goal?

Eat more bacon to celebrate. Seriously!

Skip a day on the treadmill. <<That's heaven right there, my friends.

But if YOU don't know what your goal is or how you're going to achieve it, you might as well just wander off the publishing path into the darkness right now. You can still find success, but it's harder, takes longer, costs more, and is a lot more frustrating.

If you don't start as you mean to go, you'll never know if you get to where you were meant to go.

Recap:

1. Are you being smart about your business? Genre, pricing, name, and goals.
2. Are you making business decisions with your head or your heart?
3. Do you have defined, specific, measurable, attainable, realistic, and timebound goals, with a plan of action if the goal is not being met?

Notes:

3

THE RAPID RELEASE STRATEGY

So now that you know a little bit about me—and I reserve the right to sidetrack whenever I want!—and you've defined your own genres and goals, let's get into the rapid release strategy.

This might not be a strategy everyone can handle. Everyone leads a different life, from kids to dogs to day job. I know; I have all of those. And a demanding volunteer church duty. You have stuff too. We all do.

A few questions to consider before you get too far into committing yourself to a rapid release strategy.

1. Can you reasonably write 5-10,000 words a day, five days a week? If yes, you can probably pull off a rapid release strategy in some form.

2. Can you afford to hire a cover artist or buy stock art for the covers you require?

3. Can you afford to spend time and/or money to edit, format, and produce books quickly? This includes tagline creation. Blurb writing. Editing manuscripts. Formatting the manuscript into a book. Putting the book up for sale/preorder. Creating a marketing plan for the book/series. Sending review copies. And everything else Indie authors do to send their books out there to be successful.

Most of this work is done BEFORE the first book comes out, so you need to ask yourself if you have the patience and commitment to work on a project for hours, days, and even months before you sell a single copy. This can be daunting. It can also be rewarding once that first book hits.

If you answered, "yes," or "I think I can," to all three of those questions, you can probably perform a rapid release with some measure of success. Now, what that success looks like for you?

That should be specific, measurable, attainable, realistic, and timebound. Written down for the series and for each book. Don't hate me! But the reason most teachers see some measure of success with the dozens of kids they teach each year is because we know the goal and how to get kids from Point A to Point B over the course of a school year.

You should know how to do that for your releases as an author. If you don't right now, never fear. Isn't that why you're reading this book?

If you don't set goals for each book in the rapid release, how will you know if your rapid release strategy was successful?

It's okay to write down, "I want to earn more than I spend in the first week." It's defined. It's specific. It's time-bound. And if you attain it, you succeeded.

Or "I want to earn more than I spent to produce the book within one month of release."

I also think it's important to note that goals can be adjusted at any time. I have a preorder goal for every book I put up. I monitor this weekly until I get close, and then I monitor it daily. If I make the preorder goal BEFORE the book goes live, I *alter* the preorder goal. Make it higher. Push myself to get more.

And if I fail and don't meet the goal for preorders? I might push harder at launch once the book is live. I might adjust my goals for the next book in the series. Or I might go, "Dang. What could I have done differently?"

And then I make a new plan based on what I learned. After all, you only know what you know *at that time*. You don't know what you don't know.

Once you learn something, use it. Your future self will thank you.

What Rapid Release is:

This is a publishing strategy where you "rapidly" put out books in a series in a timely fashion. Vague, right?

Well, I leave it vague, because YOU should get to decide what works for you. I've done the rapid release strategy in a multitude of ways, each with successes, failures, and lessons learned.

Later in this book, you'll get the details of each kind of release, with pros and cons, what I learned, and what I wouldn't do again. There will be numbers (data geeks, you're welcome!), thinking behind the timeline, and schedules for each.

But for right now, we're just going to be discussing what rapid release is, how to write it, and the steps you need to take to launch it well.

I've done the following:

1. Capitalize off of the Amazon 12-week preorder by rapidly releasing a new book in a series every 11 weeks. This was how Liz started. She was new to self-publishing and still unsure of her self-publishing chops. If this is where you are, this is a viable, "rapid" release strategy that

can build a beginner's backlist from zero to hero, while still giving you time to write the next book in between releases.

2. A 6-week rapid release strategy, again capitalizing off Amazon preorders and planned promotion. If you have a few books already written in your series, you can easily start the 6-week rapid release strategy without having all the books written.

3. An-every-3-week "summer series" strategy, spinning off those USA channel summer series like *Bunheads* and *Suits*. Did you know they put those shows on in the summer—when TV viewing is actually down—to keep people watching? I thought, "Why not do the same with books?"

4. And I launched a series of 6 books every 3 weeks from June – September 2017. ALL of the books were written before the first launched in this kind of strategy. This is because I'm a freak, and I can't handle writing a book, editing it, and publishing it within a month. I take more like 3-4 months to do that.

5. The next year, I took the summer series a step further and did the ultimate rapid release—a book every week. I did 3 in June on Weeks 2, 3, and 4. Took off the first week of July, and did 3

more books in weeks 2, 3, and 4 of July. I added 6 more books to the previous summer's series with this strategy, which boosted all 12 books that summer. All of these books were written before the first one came out as well.

6. Two books on the same day. I did this strategy last spring and summer with my billionaire romances. The genre was hot, and I had the books. I put out two books on the same day, and a month later, two more. A month later, two more. So really, within 8 weeks, I'd published 6 books across 3 release days. It was...interesting. If you have a backlog of books in a very hot genre, this strategy can bring in some cash, quick.

7. Once a month releases. This is where I've settled for the most part. Both of my names are now releasing once a month, with some exceptions. This is a comfortable rapid release strategy for me and my writing habits/styles, and the one that makes the most sense for me at this point in my career. I do have planned some other strategies for certain books/series based on their tropes/themes, but hey, that's called being an Indie Author.

You can really do whatever you want. I'm part of an author collaboration writing in a shared world where we release books every other Monday. It works.

If you want to release a book every week, or two, or three, or four, or five...you get the idea. You should do what works for you, based on what you have in the hopper, both in terms of creative energy to write, time, and money.

It takes all three to successfully pull off a rapid release strategy, in my experience and opinion, and I've done it six different ways.

Again, you'll get all the details of each strategy, with more details and numbers and the how-to from beginning to end for each of the above strategies.

Recap:

1. Is a rapid release strategy for you? Circle yes or no and pass back. ;) Sorry, that's from my junior high days in the late eighties. We used to have to pass notes, yo. No cell phones. No texting. Imagine that!
2. Do you have a defined and specific goal for your rapid release?
3. What type of rapid release strategy do you want to try? Once a week? Once a month?

Once a quarter? Choose it. Plan it. Own it. Win it.

Notes:

4

RAPID RELEASE SERIES SETUP

I n this section, we're going to talk about some setup items you should consider as you start your Rapid Release plan. We'll talk about titling, choosing dates, planning your writing, and length of series.

Book Titles and Series Titles:

Part of a successful Rapid Release strategy is writing in a series. It's very difficult to be quite as successful with standalones. It can be done, don't get me wrong. You have to be a master at backmatter (you should be anyway) and tying in secondary characters tightly into each book to get readers onto the next one.

I write romances that are standalones, tied together into a series based on a variety of things. Maybe they're siblings. Maybe they all work at the same place (a resort or a ranch). Maybe it's simply geographical.

No matter what, that tie is extremely important.

I recently spent about a half an hour of my night looking at a huge series of books all written by the same person. I also personally think this is essential to a successful Rapid Release strategy—*you yourself need to write all the books.*

I know, I know. 2019 is the year of collaborations. I've seen it everywhere too. I spent 2017 and almost all of 2018 writing in shared worlds and other collaborations.

They weren't helpful for me in terms I could live with. That's going to vary from person to person. I get that.

But I think the Rapid Release strategy is lucrative and successful *only* if an individual author controls all the books.

Think about it. In your current series, which book do you advertise the most? Which one leads people to the others?

The first book, right?

So if you're writing in a collaboration and you're book 4?

Uh...I don't think that's valuable. I'm sure there are exceptions to this, so don't send me nasty emails citing how wrong I am. I've been in those collaborations, and I got some of my fans to buy my Book 4. But did I get anyone else's fans?

Not really.

Readers are used to watching movies and TV shows in order. They don't come into a show on episode three or four. They start at the beginning. EVEN if you tell them they can read your Book 4 first, they might not. In my 24 months of experience, they don't about 90% of the time.

So all those authors doing "Rapid Releases" with a half-dozen authors? Good for them. I hope it's one of the exceptions. But I want the reader to go to MY NEXT BOOK after they read the first one. Not someone else's.

Mine.

Greedy?

Yeah, probably. I'm okay owning that.

So my advice would be to write your own series. Just you. Write them all. Edit them. Format them. Cover them. Get Amazon to link them into a series. You get the idea.

This section is supposed to be on titling that series, so we better talk about that. Once you have your series, you need to title it smartly. Remember how we're being smart?

This is where your knowledge of what's hot in the market right now will come in. What are other people in your genre doing? What are their series names? What do you need to convey to readers to get them to one-click buy book after book, read them quickly so they'll be ready for the next one, and convert them to lifelong fans?

That's how important the series title and book titles are.

In today's IPC (Indie Publishing Climate), which could change at any time, certain genres require certain things.

In clean romance, we're hitting readers over the head with tropes in our titles and series titles.

Big time.

Thwap, thwap, thwap—this is a second chance romance. This is a fake fiancé romance. This is a billionaire romance.

There's no guessing at what they'll get.

The cover speaks to this too, across all genres. In PNR shifter romance, we see the beast on the cover with the hot guy. In reverse harem, there's the woman with the number of men behind her. In motorcycle club romance, it's a single guy with abs for days.

Even the fonts are similar across genres, as they speak to what the reader will get.

This is called Packaging to Market, and readers want the story they expect behind that package—with a little twist. They want familiar but fresh. That's your job as an author to deliver that, and if you can do it quickly, you'll make more money and earn more readers for future works (that don't need to come out so quickly).

So choose carefully your titles and series titles, using the retailers out there to see what's already selling. After all, you want your packaging to fit the market as well as the book within.

Length of Series:

Going along with titles and series titles, you'll probably make a plan for how many books you'll be writing and releasing within the strategy. After all, if you've created a family with five brothers, that's five books. Right?

Well, sort of. You can always expand later. I did, in my Christmas in Coral Canyon series. I started with four brothers, but the fourth one married a woman that had two more sisters. The series expanded to six books right before my eyes—after the first one was out.

Is that a problem? Not if you can find the room in your production schedule to write the book, package it, and publish it. I didn't have the time, but I adjusted and made it. And that series did so well that I am once again expanding it by two books.

Now, those two books won't be part of the Rapid Release strategy (the series is already out), but I will be putting those two books out two weeks apart, creating their own mini Rapid Release strategy to add on to the existing series.

See how endless the possibilities are with Indie Publishing? What a time to be alive!

I would suggest a series of four or more books. Here's why: You want somewhere for readers to go. You're going to be spending a lot of time, energy, and money on this strategy, and it should pay off for you.

Personally, I think six books is better, but that's just based on my experiences across a wide range of strategies, over the course of almost four years. Your mileage may vary, as it will in everything discussed anywhere. This book. Another book. A Facebook group. Wherever.

The best part about being an Indie author is your ability to experiment. *If* you take good notes of what you did and how you felt about it, what numbers you saw, and what met your goals, you can learn what will work *for you* moving forward.

And it's all about what's working *for you*. Not for me.

So don't forget to take good notes. More on that later.

The longer the series is, the quicker you can draw readers to Book 1. I'm of the opinion that most Book 1's should be largely ignored until the next book comes out. You can still make money on Book 1, of course, but in our digital media binging society, if readers see they can read two books, or three, or more by the time they hear about Book 1, they're more likely to binge buy them *all*. I have an entire case study on this Tiered Launch Strategy, so don't worry! I won't leave you high and dry.

Sometimes when you release a book, people haven't gotten paid. They're not convinced they need to read it yet. Maybe you've done sales over the months/years of your career, and they think they'll just wait until the books go on sale.

Maybe their toddler screamed at just the moment the reader went to buy your book, and they forgot. I can't tell you how many times I've done that. I mean, I don't have toddlers, but a dog will ring the bell to go out, or my husband will text, or it's time for pick-up at school.

You're constantly competing for a reader's time and money. If they miss Book 1, you can catch them on Book 2 —only a few weeks later.

And then Book 3, and then 4, and then 5...

The room for growth is exponential with each book in a Rapid Release strategy.

That series I mentioned in the last section? It had 26 books in it, with 2 more on preorder. And those preorders were doing WELL. Like Top 1000 well—for a preorder at full price (these were $3.99).

That author has figured out the secret sauce to get people flipping pages—they were also a Kindle All-Star Author. I know. I could see it listed right there on their product page, and that's something Amazon does for those authors who earn the KU All-Star title, and it changes every month.

They were writing good books—we'll talk about this later too. They were putting them out quickly. I believe the first book came out in 2015, and they're now on Book 26, with some spin-off series in there as well.

This series grows each month, and people are hungry for it.

Now, I'm not saying you need a huge, massive 26-book series. But what I'm saying is the more books you have, the more potential for growth and income you have. So don't skimp.

Think big.

And then get ready to write.

. . .

Planning Your Production Schedule:

If you don't have a production schedule for your Rapid Release, you'll likely fail. I'm just going to say that up front. Planning is essential in writing for a Rapid Release. Everyone has comfort levels with their writing and publishing, so what I say might not apply to you.

But for me, I need to be 2-3 months ahead of my release date to be comfortable. That's a *need* for me, and I've learned that over the six years I've been self-publishing.

So you get to decide what you need to be comfortable when writing, editing, proofing, formatting, covering, packaging, and publishing your books.

Being an Indie Author is so much more than just drafting. This is fortunate and unfortunate, depending on how you look at it.

If you don't know your routine yet, learn it first. I've been tracking my word count for over a year now. I know the exact number of words I've written per day over the last 18 months. This helped me learn how many days off I needed each month. It helped me see trends in my own productivity. It helped me know how long it took me to write a chapter, a novella, a book, and more.

It's my belief that you need to know those things about yourself before you can make a production schedule for your Rapid Release.

For example, I know I can write a 55,000-word cowboy romance in twelve days. That's two weeks, with Sundays off, and only 5000 words/day.

I don't mean that to sound disparaging. "Only 5000 words/day." But I learned over time that I can easily write three chapters a day, and that's between 5000-6000 words per day. And at that rate, with a couple of days at a slightly higher rate, I can finish a book in twelve days.

That's two weeks.

So technically, I could release one book, write the next, and release it two weeks later. Just thinking about that leaves me in a pile of goo, quivering with anxiety. It's not how I operate. I need more flexibility than that. I have a family and other obligations, and writing is *not* my life.

Oh...what did I just say?

Writing is not my life.

I have so much more to my life, and I need to be able to live that life *in addition to* being a writer. That's another lesson I learned early in my career. I won't go into it here. But it helps me form my production schedule, because I refuse to be left behind in my family life, my church life, my real life, just to write my books.

If that works for you, that's fine. You should know that and be able to use your production schedule as such.

So I would counsel you to plan your production wisely, based on your own personality, your family life and other obligations, and what you've learned about how you work/write/publish.

Look at your calendar with your book series beside you. What are you going to do? Once a month? Every 6 weeks?

How fast can you write a book? How many do you need written to be comfortable before the first one drops?

How long does your packaging take? This is everything to get the book ready after you've written THE END on the first draft. Editing, proofing, formatting, getting or making a cover. Writing a blurb. Setting up launch marketing. Newsletter swaps. Preorders or not?

There are dozens of variables, and you need a grip on all of them *before* Book 1 hits the virtual shelves.

I would give yourself at least thirty days after packaging of Book 1 to do launch prep. During that time, you can of course be writing another book, but nothing should be waiting to be done on that first book. Just marketing, so you can hit the ground at full speed and give your Rapid Release strategy the best chance of success.

With the calendar open and all of this knowledge in your back pocket, put your drafting dates on the calendar at a comfortable rate for you, remembering you need time to package after the draft is done.

This will give you a good idea of when your first release date can be.

Put that on the calendar too. Remember that adjustments can be made to almost anything—as long as you don't do a preorder, that is.

Now I did all of my Rapid Releases over the years with preorders. I thrive on the deadline part of it. If that doesn't work for you, and you're worried you might need wiggle room, don't be afraid to take it.

Then get ready to write—and I have strategies to help you write faster in the next chapter.

Recap:

1. Research the market so you know how to title your books and your series. Make sure your packaging fits the market for your genre to a T.

2. How long will your series be? Make a plan for it BEFORE you start writing, then you can plan your production schedule. Don't forget to think big when it comes to series. At least four books, maybe more.

3. Plan your production schedule for everything it takes to get a book from a blank page to publication. Use a calendar and don't be afraid to adjust if necessary.

Notes:

5

WRITING IN A RAPID RELEASE STRATEGY

Okay. #cracksknuckles

Hopefully, you've had a lot to think about already. Did you think there was so much to a Rapid Release strategy? Maybe you did. Maybe you didn't. Either way, I hope you've been empowered to do things the way you want to do them. I hope you've set some goals and have an idea of how YOU work as an author.

Now, it's time to write.

I think there are strategies for writing books you're looking to Rapid Release that you wouldn't do with every book. However, over time, you might like the process so much that it *does* become what you do for every book. That's fine too.

What you're going to do with a Rapid Release book is write fast, from beginning to end. That's it.

Don't go back and edit. Leave yourself a note and move on.

And maybe we better back up a step. As you start writing your first book, you should send an email to your team as well. This includes a cover designer, editor, proof-readers, betas (if you use them), formatter, and maybe take out a monthly subscription to whatever gets you through the day.

Bacon of the month club, maybe? I mean, everyone needs some positive affirmation when writing in a Rapid Release strategy. Maybe coffee is what you need. Steak? Alcohol!

No matter what, get your team in place so you can get the most words laid down on a day-to-day basis and still stay human. Or mostly human.

A few things first—I know! I keep telling you we'll get to the writing, and we still haven't gotten there! But we will.

Outlining is key.

If you do not have a current outlining strategy, I daresay you are not quite ready to write this way. Now, don't go all panther on me and start throwing Coke cans. I started in this industry in 2007 and I was a self-proclaimed pantser. I did not outline.

The very thought made me shiver. I wrote many books this way. All of my traditionally published books were not outlined. I've always been a fast writer, but I am a very slow editor/reviser.

I wrote my first traditionally published book in 18 days. It was 90,000 words. It then took me nine months to revise it into something I felt like I could send out and put my name on.

NINE MONTHS.

Well, friends, you do not have nine months to revise your book in a Rapid Release strategy. You just don't.

You need to be able to work faster than that.

Over the years, as I continued to write, as I moved from one genre to another, I learned how to outline. I personally love several methods I've tried and used and have meshed all into one big spreadsheet I use now. I've heavily borrowed from many other authors, and I've come up with things for myself as well.

Right now, I use a mixture of Blake Snyder's Save the Cat for screenwriters, combined with some other things I use to build characters. This is the best story structure I've found. It just resonates with me. I've used Dan Wells's Seven-Point Story Structure as well.

I adore and use Gwen Hayes's *Romancing the Beat* structure, and I downloaded and use Jami Gold's Beat Sheet for romance writers (a spin-off of Blake Snyder's beat sheets) as the basis of my outlining.

I have about 6 tabs at the bottom of that sheet now, with scads of character and series information. I don't create a new spreadsheet for each book. I simply DUPLICATE it and save it as a new name. (In Excel, it's as simple as SAVE AS and giving it the name of your next book in the series. Then all your character info for previous characters is there. Your map is there. Your series info is there. EVERYTHING is there.)

Yes, I make a map of my town. Sometimes of the buildings my people live, if they're significant. Then I don't have to waste any time trying to remember what the name of the street was where the diner is. Or what the diner's called.

And I don't know about you, but I'm getting old now, and I can't keep all of that in my head from book to book, while being a mom, a taxi driver, a wife, a cook, and writing 10K/day.

Fine, I don't cook.

But everything else takes a LOT of brainpower. So let your spreadsheet carry some of that weight for you.

With this spreadsheet, I have ALL the info I need with only two clicks. As I research things, I put the links in the spreadsheet. Then I don't have to waste time finding them again later. I can make notes for future books as ideas come to me. I can write the tagline/blurb right there in the spreadsheet.

Literally, everything is there. You can find the spreadsheet on my website, which is listed in the Resources at the end of this book.

When you look at that, you'll see this is more than an outline. This is a character Bible. I know what my characters look like, who their friends are, what they like/dislike, all of it. I know what their issues are, what triggers them, their past relationships, their family background, their professional background.

All. Of. It.

I can fill out a spreadsheet like this over the course of about three hours. Then I'm ready to write. And I don't do it all at once. I generally start characterizing and outlining about halfway through the previous book I'm writing, so when I finish one on Tuesday, I'm ready to start writing the next book on Wednesday morning.

And I get up at 5 a.m. on Wednesdays, and nobody has time for outlining that early. If I'm giving up sleep, it's for WORDS.

But that's just me.

Work is work, right? It all needs to be done.

Anyway, back to outlining. I think it's worth your time to invest in it. It will help you write faster. It will help you write cleaner. And you need to do both in a Rapid Release strategy.

Determine book length.

I've done all lengths of books in a Rapid Release. My longer books are between 50-55,000 words and I've done them on 11-week, 6-week, and monthly releases.

My shorter books are 30-40,000 words, and I've done

them on 3-week, weekly, and twice in one day releases (as well as monthly).

The length of your book doesn't really matter, though it does affect your production schedule and your pricing. But if you know how much you can write, on average, in a given week, you can plan your production schedule around the length of your books.

Again, don't be afraid to make adjustments. If you find yourself falling behind, one tactic to keep up or get caught up is to shorten your books a little later in the series. I wouldn't advise this unless you were in a dire place, though—like about to lose your preorder status on Amazon—because readers expect a certain length of book from an author after a while.

Determine deadlines.

Now that you have an idea of when your books will be coming out, and when you'll be writing them, it's time to live by the deadlines.

Especially if you've chosen to do preorders. You don't want to get in trouble with Amazon and/or make fans angry by missing those deadlines. You need to have your final manuscript uploaded three days before the book goes live in an Amazon preorder, and they operate on the UTC time zone. So make adjustments accordingly.

I actually schedule out all my deadlines. I'm drafting books about 3 months ahead of their publication date.

Sometimes farther. Before I start drafting, I almost always have a cover ready. So that piece is in place.

I have my editor and proofreader ready, and they need my book when I say I'm going to give it to them. They have other clients, you know?

So I get the drafting done, get the book out to the team. I focus on other things—and heaven knows there are a million+one things you can be doing in Indie Publishing.

On or about the first of each month, I look at what's coming out in the next month. So about January 1, I look at what February holds for me. I edit the books I have back from my editing/proofing team, format them, and get them out to my ARC team and up on Amazon.

This might take me the whole month to do, depending on how many releases I have in February. This past February, I had 4. Four book releases. That's a lot to manage. I do it around drafting of other books, and it seems to work for me.

You should know your system. If you don't have one, you need to get one. I have deadlines for everything, and I keep track of everything in a spreadsheet. This way, there aren't books getting dropped and things not getting done on time.

I put all of those dates—when a book is going out for proofing, when it needs to be formatted, when it goes to the ARC team, when it needs to be uploaded for final publication—on the spreadsheet.

Then I don't miss deadlines.

Write it!

Okay, you've got your production schedule down. You've named dates you're publishing. You've determined deadlines. You have your team on-call for you. Things are happening!

This is *really* happening.

Now it's time to get the books written. You might have some leeway in your schedule, where some of the books will be out as you write the later ones. That's fine. But no matter what, you've got to have some strategies for getting words down quickly.

I said this earlier, but you're definitely going to need to outline at least a little bit. Write from beginning to end, with no editing in between. And know how much you can tolerate on any given day.

Paul J. Meyer said, "Productivity is never an accident. It is always the result of a commitment to excellence, intelligent planning, and focused effort."

You've got the commitment down. You've planned.

Now it's time to focus.

Here a several more strategies to help you focus and get more words written:

1. **Write first.** I learned this from Skye Warren, where

she says she only has a limited amount of time to write. And she learned to write first. Not after the emails were checked, or after the Facebook groups were looked at, or after the ad work was done. But write first.

2. Set a goal for the day. For me, this is usually a word count goal, and I break it into however many sessions I have that day (between 1 – 4 usually). So if the goal is 5000 words, and I have 3 writing sessions, I try for 2000 words each session.

3. Split up your day. I can't focus or be creative for longer than about 1.5 hours. So I set my writing blocks of time to 90 minutes. In that time, I have certain goals (see #2 above), and I work toward them.

4. Eliminate distractions as much as possible during writing time. I know a lot of moms who are writers. You can't just eliminate your kids! LOL. I get it. So as you're segmenting up your day, eliminate distractions DURING THAT TIME.

So maybe your kids are at school, or you've arranged playdates, or you can put a movie on. Just try to eliminate as many distractions as you can.

For me, after I retired from teaching, I found myself distracted by housework. Which was odd, because I did the bare minimum while I was teaching, taxiing, momming, and writing. So why now, was I suddenly feeling like I needed to mop the floors or clean the bathrooms?

I knew why. I was home, and I wanted my husband to

see that I had done something valuable that day. Yes, I know my writing is valuable, but it's also unseen. So I found myself cleaning all the time.

And the goal of my retirement was not to clean. It was to write. So I hired a housekeeper, and now my mental energy is freed up to write. I know the house will get cleaned—every Tuesday.

5. Play to your strengths. Are you really good at dialog? Push yourself to go faster during those times. Save an action scene for your first scene of the day, because you're good at those and they get the words flowing.

6. Stop writing in the middle of a sentence. Then when you come back next time, be it that same day or the next, you can pick right up where you left off.

7. Schedule time off. I never write on Sunday, and I generally have between 8-10 days off each month. That's right, I only write for two-thirds of the month! I still lay down huge word counts, because I can be more productive on writing days if my creative well is full.

8. Push yourself. How many words can you typically write in a day? Push yourself to write 500 per day more for a week. Then make that your new goal.

9. Get up 30 minutes earlier or stay up 30 minutes later and see what you can do. Focused attention on writing only during that half-hour.

10. Train yourself to write in shorter blocks of time. Even 15 minutes can be 500 words. Set a timer. Use an app. Sprint with a friend. Just try it! You won't know if you like it or can do it until you try. Discard what doesn't work for you. Keep what does.

11. Go somewhere new to write. I have a friend who loves to write at the hospital. I was like, "Wait...what?" She claims it's quiet there. No one bothers her. There's WiFi. Hey, to each her own, you know? I've gone to the library. I've taken my laptop to the park while the dogs play. I write in the car on my steering wheel desk. Change it up. Get the creativity flowing.

12. Reward yourself for small benchmarks. We do this all the time with kids. Adults are just like kids, especially when it comes to being motivated to work. If you love chocolate covered raisins, only give yourself one for every page you write. Or every 100 words. Whatever will get your fingers moving.

13. Try dictation. I've heard it works well for a lot of people. I tried it a while ago, and wow. It does not fit my life. I have dogs in and out, the TV on, kids texting, calling, or asking me questions, and a husband who can't find anything. LOL. But yeah. Me having a quiet space for dictating? Nope. Doesn't happen. So I'm a typer.

14. Walk away if things aren't working. That's right. Get up and do something else for a while. The ideas will come back. They'll flow again. You might just need a break—so take one!

15. Talk out sticky plot points with a friend/partner/spouse.

. . .

No matter how you get the words on the page, just get them down. Trust your team. Outline the next book.

Recap:

1. Outlining is key to having a quick draft.
2. Determine your book length and establish deadlines to finish and publish the books.
3. Put your team on alert for covers, editing, and proofing. Create deadlines for formatting and uploading as well, in an organizational system that works well for you.
4. Write!

Notes:

6

RAPID RELEASE BEHIND-THE-SCENES SETUP

I've found that the behind-the-scenes setup in a Rapid Release strategy can make or break your success. These are all the little details you need to have in line in order to publish and launch a book well.

There are book descriptions (cover copy, which, hey, I have an Indie Inspiration book coming called Writing Killer Cover Copy), taglines, titles, series titles, subtitles, covers, and then marketing strategies.

Some of these you can employ your team to take care of, like covers. I'd find the ones that are selling well in the genre where I want to sell well and send those to my designer. If you're the designer, you'd do the same thing. I don't do my own covers. There are some things I know I'm good at, and some things I know I'm not.

Playing to your strengths for the win!

You need really good taglines and cover copy. I'm not

going to spend much time talking about these here, because I devoted an entire book to them you can check out. I think you need to have these things well-established a week or two before release if you're not doing preorders, and definitely solid and set in stone before the preorder goes live if you are doing preorders.

I've spent a lot of years polling my newsletter subscribers—I have about 40,000 of them—and the top two things they look at when deciding to buy a book or not are the cover and the description. So spending time and effort and money on those two things to get it right can help you sell more books, have a better launch, and make your Rapid Release strategy be more successful.

Your titles, subtitles, and series titles should be given careful consideration as well. Look at your genre again. I recently rebranded eight books in a series that had titles like "Before the Leap" and "After the Fall" because they no longer fit in the market.

The Indie market changes a lot too, so if you've been around awhile, it's worth looking at what's selling right now and seeing if you can't make your books fit into those slots a little bit better. For me, my books already fit in the slots.

But they weren't titled like they did. I didn't just change the title to something that didn't work with the story inside. I strategically chose what would fit the book and the market, hired a new designer, and invested in my backlist.

So while you should do this up-front for your Rapid Release, it's a strategy you can continue to employ throughout your career. After all, the work you've already done on your backlist shouldn't go to waste, right?

What I'd really like to focus on in this chapter is a Rapid Release marketing strategy. What I'm going to say might be a little revelatory to you. Whenever I get questions from authors, they're usually a breath away from burning out. They're frustrated. They feel like they're working 15 hours a day—and many of them are!—and not really getting the results they want.

The reason for this? They're focusing on TOO MUCH. That seems contrary to what you might think. If I focus on every release, every launch, every book, won't every book sell better?

The answer is no.

And you'll find yourself a puddle on the couch, wondering why you're working ninety-hour weeks and not seeing the fruits of that. Besides insanity, sleep-deprivation, and family strife, that is.

So stop doing that.

I propose to you a different way of looking at launches. The big, over-arching idea is this: Not all launches are created equal.

Stop believing those voices out there telling you that if you don't launch a book well, you've failed and there's nothing you can do.

They're wrong.

And what does "well" mean, anyway?

I just don't believe that. I don't, because I've seen the proof that contradicts it time and again in my own career, and remember, I've been around since 2007.

So it's time to start launching your Rapid Release. This means you've already put in all the work to draft the books, edit and revise them, cover them, proofread them. You've written killer descriptions and taglines and have ad copy ready to go.

Oh, did I not mention anything about ad copy? Well, depending on which type of ads you're planning for your releasing you'll need ad copy. I like to prepare mine in advance. That way, once my book is live, I can set up ads in 30 minutes or less.

So Amazon Advertising gives you 150 characters, and I like to have something that fits the tagline I've written. In fact, I usually use my tagline. But I don't want to waste time, so I prep all of this in advance. Same for Facebook ads. Same for any and all graphics I might need for FB ads or BookBub ads.

Now, I don't run all of these on every launch, or I'd be broke and blubbering, remember? But for any promotions or marketing strategies that involve advertising, I prep all of this stuff in advance. It's part of your pre-launch behind-the-scenes setup that shouldn't be overlooked.

You've spent money, time, and energy, probably a substantial amount of all of those, on everything up to this point.

And you haven't made a dime yet.

This is why the Rapid Release strategy isn't for everyone. But remember how you asked yourself those questions back in Chapter 3? That was one of them. You either answered "Yes," or "I think I can," to those questions, or you wouldn't be in this chapter.

Now, it's time to release the books.

How do you go about doing it?

I think the best way is in a tiered format, especially if you release often. I still do this in my once/month release strategy, because hey, releasing once a month IS a Rapid Release! It is. So not every launch is created equally.

I don't have the same budget of time, money, and energy for each release. I time things to when I want to push them, and I use the work I've already done (past releases = my backlist) to earn money all the time.

I am not dependent on my next book to pay my bills. I don't want to be. Work I've already done is how I pay my bills.

And I do that by employing a Tiered Release Strategy. I've been doing this type of strategy for about three years now. I just didn't realize it until I saw scads of new authors enter my genre and start releasing books.

See, writing fast used to be something I was very good at. I mean, I'm still good at it, but I was one of the *few* people that were good at it. Not so anymore. Things change, and suddenly in this new IPC, there were dozens and dozens of people releasing a book every month.

How can I compete? One of my strengths was no longer "special."

I started watching everyone. It was a hard 15 months, I'm not going to lie. I saw things I didn't agree with. I heard things I had direct proof to the contrary. I saw and heard people do and say things I didn't think were even ethical.

But through it all, I realized I was still doing something different from them, and that was my launch strategy. Now, no matter where you are in your career, you're going to be making more than some people and less than others.

Another revelation: Money is not the sole indicator of one's success. I know in our current IPC, we think it is. It's not.

But I was making a lot of money doing what I do, and I wasn't burning out. I'm still writing upwards of 200,000-250,000 words each month, and that's with several days off. I only spend one hour each day on marketing. I enjoy going to the park, walking the dogs, getting on the treadmill, and watching reality TV.

In short, I have a life. I'm not working 15 hours a day, and I think a lot of that is more valuable than money.

Anyway, I digress. I said I would! I mean, who actually likes getting on the treadmill?

Let's talk about a Tiered Launch Strategy. It sounds exactly like what it is: A launch strategy that has levels.

There's a top level launch, a medium level launch, and

a low level launch. I call them Hard, Medium, and Soft. We're the Three Bears!

I rank them as follows:

1 – Hard

2 – Medium

3 – Soft

A Tier 1, Hard Launch means I'm going to put a ton into it. I'm going to spend money advertising. I'm going to segment my newsletter list. I'm going to set up swaps. I'm going to buy outside services. I'm going to (probably) put previous books or future books or the book itself on sale.

The other tiers don't get as much as Tier 1, in varying degrees. I'll explain more. Keep reading!

Here's why you should consider creating a Tiered Release Strategy:

1. You need a break. Readers need a break. *Everyone* needs a break. You constantly pushing a new book at them month after month—or more than that—is exhausting for everyone. No wonder you don't feel like writing.

No wonder your ads are barely breaking even. I mean, NO WONDER.

So what? you're saying. Don't you want your books to sell, Elana?

Yes. Yes, I do. And I want yours to sell as well. Which is why you need to give people a break, yourself included.

You simply can't maintain the excitement and energy needed to push every new release like you do your top tier books.

2. Using a Tiered Release Strategy allows you to put marketing money toward your backlist. That's your bread and butter, not the shinier new book that's out there.

This might cause a mind shift for you. But think about it. Wouldn't you rather make money on what you've ALREADY done instead of relying on your newest book to pay the bills?

I would. In fact, I make 90% of my monthly income on the work I've ALREADY done. That's my backlist at work.

Does this mean I ignore my new releases?

Wait for it... *Yes. Some of them.* The third tier to be more exact. Those books come out with little to no fanfare as I push backlist books and lay in wait to attack readers when I want them to buy.

Mwaa ha ha!

That sounds terrible. I don't actually attack readers. But I do market books to them at strategic times and it's NOT ALWAYS upon release.

So what is a Tiered Release Strategy?

It's one where you look at all the books you have coming out this year. If you don't know that, make the list now. I do this in September or October of the previous year, and I have release dates set up for the next calendar year. Titles. Everything.

Then I assign each book a ranking. Either a 1 for a Hard release. 2 for Medium. 3 for Soft, as I outlined earlier.

Books that are assigned a 1 get a lot of marketing dollars and push right when they come out. These are generally Book 2s in a new series, and then Book 5 or 6 (or both) in that same series.

Not Book 1? you ask.

Nope. It's my opinion that Book 1s in a new series for an author, even established ones, should be Medium releases, if not Low.

I can hear your jaws dropping. *What's your reasoning?* you ask.

Experience. My pen name makes almost $50,000/month by herself. She has 60 books in her back-list and releases a new book once/month. 2 series a year.

Even for her, Book 1 is a harder sell. People are leery of the new series. Will they like it as well as XYZ series that they're SURE is their favorite?

Unknown. Maybe they'll wait for Book 2 or 3 to come out, especially if you've got a reputation of putting Book 1 on sale as subsequent books come out (which I do).

Authors also get stressed when Book 1 in a new series comes out...and doesn't do as well as they hoped.

It can really take the wind out of your sails. You feel depressed. Maybe your readership isn't as big as you though it was. You should stop writing. Hey, there's a new documentary on Netflix. Etc, etc.

But you can avoid those negative thought patterns if you've *planned* for the book to simply come out and do whatever it's going to do.

Does this mean I never push Book 1 in a new series?

Nope, I have done that and will continue to do it. In fact, I just released a new romantic suspense series. I've never done romantic suspense before, and I wanted to make a big splash. Book 1 was a Hard Release, and I pushed it, and pushed it, and pushed it.

But there is no way I have enough money, time, and energy to do that for EVERY book in that series—they came out every 2 weeks! No way. Can't happen. I'd be broke, exhausted, and wondering how this is now my life.

If you're there, don't worry! You can change how you do things in your author business. Maybe start with taking a long, hard look at what you're spending your money, time, and energy doing, and do something different.

Like your launch strategy.

Truth: A book does not earn all of its money the first day it comes out. That's the beauty of Indie Publishing and a digital backlist that takes up no shelf space.

So stop thinking like that.

The last case study in this book outlines the Tiered

Release Strategy with Liz Isaacson's Cowboy Billionaires, where you can see how a Tiered Release Strategy really paid off.

I think a Tiered Release Strategy is a key component of any Rapid Release strategy, and you'll be doing yourself a huge favor to take some time to plan such a Tiered Release Strategy well before that first book in your Rapid Release comes out.

Recap:

1. There is much to prepare for a Rapid Release. Getting your ducks in a row with regards to blurbs/cover copy, taglines, covers, titles, and marketing strategies should not be skipped over.

2. A Tiered Release Strategy is essential for Rapid Releasers who don't want to burn out.

Notes:

7

LAUNCHING THE RAPID RELEASE

Okay! You've written the books. You've exercised those muscles to be a faster, leaner, and meaner author than you were before.

Great! You have everything planned...almost. There's still a lot to do for the launch of your Rapid Release. Let's talk about a few things that I think are essential in ensuring success. Remember, everything I've done in specific Rapid Release strategies (once/month, once/week, etc.) will be discussed and laid out for you in just a couple of more chapters! Hang in there.

To Preorder or Not to Preorder:

I feel like this is a chicken-or-egg scenario. Or KU-vs-Wide. We can debate it for-freaking-ever and reach no conclusion. I honestly don't care what you decide to do for your Rapid Release.

I've had success both ways, but I am a primarily pro-preorder author. I put 90% of my books on preorder.

Here's why: I like making money. LOL. I know you do too. And I know TONS of authors doing a Live Launch (no preorder) who would be willing to argue with me that they make money too.

I know they do.

So, really, either one will work.

The decision should be made based on how you mean to go. Remember that chapter about starting as you mean to go?

I started with full-priced ($2.99 or $3.99) preorders. That's how I've gone. My readership expects that.

If you launch every book at 99¢, you will be building a readership that expects you to launch every book at 99¢.

Start as you mean to go.

Changing the pricing structure and preorder structure for your existing readers is not easy. But really, nothing about Indie Publishing is all that easy, so hopefully you thought, *Challenge accepted!*

I put all of this here to basically say, Do what you think will work for you. For your existing readership/fan-base. For the genre you're putting the books out in. To help you achieve the goals you wrote and set earlier in this book.

If you believe a preorder will help with achieving the

goals you've set, do a preorder. If you don't think it will, don't do a preorder.

You do have to have things ready sooner for a preorder. Blurbs, taglines, titles, covers, and you can't miss the deadline to upload your manuscript. So keep all of that in mind.

Graphics:

I make graphics for all of my launches, whether they be Hard, Medium, or Soft. I do these typically 6 weeks out from release (if it's a preorder), and make final adjustments/new graphics the week before as well.

If you have a sale on previous books, you need graphics. If you're announcing a new series out every 2 weeks, you need graphics. You need launch graphics. You need header graphics for Facebook or your newsletter and websites. You might make teaser graphics.

What I'm saying is schedule some time to make graphics. I've used Canva, PicMonkey, and BookBrush for these. I like PicMonkey and BookBrush the best. Your mileage may vary, and maybe you know PhotoShop. Maybe you'll hire this out.

Whatever you do, get some good graphics to help with your launches, with building excitement from book to book, and with establishing the foundation for a successful Rapid Release.

· · ·

Utilizing social media:

Social media is used in every tier of a Rapid Release strategy. I always put up graphics and links for my releases, at the bare minimum. I don't boost or pay for any posts in my Softer launches, but you get to decide what a Soft launch means to you.

If you have reader groups, link to your post on your page, or link to the book. If you have a Review Crew, utilize them to get up reviews.

I don't think posting the same thing over and over in the scads of groups on Facebook works that well anymore. I'm sure there are people who think it does or have proof that it does. To me, it's not where I'm choosing to spend my time and energy.

I post five days a week (and sometimes more) on my author page on Facebook. I ask my readers a lot of questions there, and I go like and respond to their comments. That's where I choose to focus, and I get good engagement from posts on a page, including the ones about my newest release.

Utilizing your NL:

For a Rapid Release launch, I like to segment my newsletter. This helps me avoid a spike on the very first day, which is naturally going to happen. Depending on the type of release, I'll segment into 2 groups, 3 groups, or 5 groups. I've sent out over the course of 5 days (one group each day for 5 days), and I've sent out staggered emails over the course of 2-3 days (2 groups on day 1, 3 groups go out on day 2, etc.).

No matter what, your mailing list is your warmest audience. They're the closest to you, and they've assumedly signed up to hear from you. Use them. Sell to them.

Now, if you don't have a big list, all is not lost. The huge booms of mailing lists from 2016 and 2017 are mostly over, so if you're just getting in the pool now, you might feel like you're drowning.

You're not.

There are some genres out there where mailing list subscribers are still just as hungry, and there are some that aren't.

If you want to actively grow your list, you probably need to give them something. A reader magnet, this is called, and it can be anything, from a novella to bonus excerpt from the book they just finished reading.

That's up to you, and I'm not going to go into detail here about how to grow your list. If you have one, you might consider segmenting it for releases to spread out sales, either throughout a few days, or several.

Utilizing other authors:

Depending on the tier of launch you're planning, you might set up newsletter swaps, social media shares, or

Facebook group takeovers as part of your launch strategy. This requires connections with other authors you know and trust, and they can be a great way to reach more readers than you currently have in your fanbase.

I would typically only do these for Medium or Hard launches, as it's a lot of work to coordinate events, schedules, swaps, and other things. You have to reciprocate down the line, which is more of your time and energy. And remember, you only have so much time and energy to spare before you're that pile of goo on the couch, ready to quit writing and wonder if people make a living weaving baskets.

Yeah, basket-weaving sounds fun about this time in your life.

Don't go there.

Don't be a basket-weaver because you're spending too much time and energy on the wrong marketing techniques at the wrong time.

Notice I didn't say they were wrong ALL the time. But there's a definite time and place to pull out all the stops—and it's NOT on every book.

Unless you like basket-weaving....

Utilizing your other books:

The most natural thing to do to use your other books to launch one or more books within a Rapid Release strategy is to lower the price on one or more of them.

If you've launched at full price, you have a couple of steps to go: 99¢ or free. I'd step down one at a time, saving my biggest sale (free) for when I have the most books out, for the maximum sell-through potential.

It generally looks like this:

Book 1 – Medium release. I get it out there at full price and let it gather in my existing fanbase.

Book 2 – Hard release. Set Book 1 to 99c. Advertise the series.

Book 3, 4, and 5 – Soft releases. Get the books out at full price. Keep building, telling your NL, posting on social media.

Book 6 – Hard release. Set Book 1 to free (if in KU). Put other books at 99¢, possibly even this brand new Book 6. Push everything with as much as you have.

That's a general outline. I don't do this every time. Sometimes I put Book 1 at 99¢ and push it with everything I have. I typically do this if my books are releasing close together, in a popular genre, or I really want to get readers into the series so they'll preorder at full price after devouring that one book.

This takes a very strong Book 1. It takes voracious readers. It takes some nerves of steel, because I literally have NO read-through to pull in money I'm spending.

There are a lot of strategies. Hopefully by the time you

go through my case studies, you'll have an idea of what you want to try.

Recap:

1. Decide if you'll do preorders or not.
2. Label all of your launches and start to prep how you'll use your own newsletter list, other authors and their lists/groups/contacts, your previous books, and your social media. These are things you have to build as you're writing and publishing. So plan posts on your social media, get subscribers, and/or make connections.
3. Be sure to schedule some time for graphic creation.
4. Seriously consider basket-weaving...not! You can do this!

Notes:

8

DETERMINING SUCCESS IN RAPID RELEASE

Your success in a Rapid Release depends on the goals you set for yourself. Perhaps you simply want to see if you can take a book from blank pages to a packaged product faster. Once you have that process down, maybe you'd like to up your income. Maybe you'd like to try different release strategies and see what works for you.

No matter what you choose as your goal, break it down into manageable chunks. Remember, it should be specific, manageable, attainable, realistic, and time-bound.

And you'll need to track the numbers in your Rapid Release. There are various ways to do this, even something as simple as a Google sheet or an Excel file. I use those as I'm going through the Rapid Release, but then I use an online tool called ReaderLinks to look at things in an easier, big-picture way.

You can use something like ReaderLinks or BookReport, but I like ReaderLInks more. It has the capability to group books into series, which is beneficial for me. And I can put in my ad spend from FB and AMS, which shows me how much I spent to make the money I did.

Because you want a positive ROI (return-on-investment) with anything you're doing with regards to advertising. And since you should have a marketing strategy for your Rapid Release, you're likely going to have some ad spend.

If you don't, that's fine too. But you should track your numbers. After all, data doesn't lie.

I've put together a very simple Rapid Release Tracker, and it's basically just a way to keep track of sales, pagereads, income, spend, and your profit/loss. Hopefully, you'll see an increase in the numbers as the books come out, remembering not to let negative thought patterns derail you on Soft launches. Find it on the resources page on my website: http://elanajohnson.com/resources

Recap:

1. Data doesn't lie. Keep track of your numbers. If you don't do it as you go, use a way to go back in time and get the numbers you need.
2. Numbers don't lie. How did you do compared to your goal? Was it successful?

3. What did you learn for next time? New strategies to try? Something you wish you'd done? Make notes of that and be ready to try again!

Notes:

9

RAPID RELEASE DEBRIEF

W hew! This Rapid Release isn't for the faint of heart, is it? There's a ton of work that goes into it, but there can be a ton of profit as well.

I'll just say that I really like the Rapid Release strategy, in case that wasn't obvious throughout the book. I like it, because it plays to one of my strengths, which is writing fast. I also like it, because I really enjoy the experimentation aspect of being an Indie author.

I love trying new things and seeing what works. I like experimenting with different ad platforms and audiences, and I like seeing if I can find one that will really move books for me. I like interacting with readers, and I love helping authors.

So the Rapid Release strategy gives me plenty of opportunities to do all of those things, while still enjoying the process.

. . .

A note about data:

Data is hard numbers. As you flip to the next section, you're going to see hard numbers. They don't lie.

I love numbers. In teaching, we use them to drive our instruction. To drive our tier 1 interventions to make sure all students are learning. To identify which students have already learned and are ready to move on.

Numbers don't lie. That bears repeating. It can be hard to know with 100% certainty if a particular strategy worked, because you can't release the same book over again, with only one modification to test.

Some books sell better because of cover or trope. But I've set those things aside as variables I can't control. The margin of error, I call it.

And I look at the numbers. What are they telling me? What did I do with a particular release/launch or with a series that helped me accomplish my goal?

I hope you have a goal.

I'll state that mine is to make the most money I can. So my business model is run on profit/loss. What can I do to make the most money? What launches do that for me? What strategies did I employ? What did I do that didn't seem to work?

And how will I know?

Numbers.

It's all about the numbers.

The data.

If you aren't tracking the data somehow, how will you know? I'm not as detailed as some. I don't have long spreadsheets with daily numbers. I do monthly reports with read-through numbers, as well as sales/pages read, along with notes of what promotions I did for that particular series/launch.

That's it.

Data is important. If you're not tracking your data somehow, you should be.

I'm simple. I use ReaderLinks (paid service), and Google Sheets. Everything is online, accessible from my phone if I need it. That's it.

Recap:

1. Once you've completed a Rapid Release strategy, evaluate. Did you like it? Why or why not?
2. Would you try it again? Why or why not?
3. Which strategies need tweaking for next time? What ideas do you have for next time? Start planning!
4. Did you meet your initial goal? Did you have to adjust it as you went? Why? What is another goal you'd like to achieve with a Rapid Release?

5. Are you keeping track of your data? How?
   What methods work for you? If not, set a goal
   to start tracking your numbers so you know if
   you're hitting your goals.

Notes:

10

RAPID RELEASING EVERY 11 WEEKS - CASE STUDY 1

O kay, let's dive into the case studies. For this one, we're going to look at 16 months of data, starting with Book 1 in the Three Rivers Ranch Romance series by Liz Isaacson, and ending with Book 9 in that same series. (The series has more books now, but the last 5 came later, and weren't part of this Rapid Release strategy.)

The time line goes from September 2015 – December 2016. During this time, my pen name of Liz Isaacson released a new book in the Three Rivers Ranch Romance series every 11 weeks.

All of the books were released at full price, except the last one in December 2016. Full price for this series was $3.99.

All of the books had full 12-week preorders on Amazon.

All of the books were in Kindle Unlimited.

Liz was a brand new author, with no previous publications, no website, no blog, no newsletter. I did tell people that it was me, and Elana Johnson had a meager fanbase in young adult science fiction and fantasy, which is a far cry from Christian cowboy romance, which is what the Three Rivers Ranch Romance series was.

So let's look at the numbers!

September 2015: Book 1, Second Chance Ranch, comes out on September 15.

I pretty much didn't know how to market a book. There was no Amazon Marketing Services. I didn't yet know about Facebook ads.

I was a brand new author, with not many resources. I didn't have a newsletter yet. All I had was this one book, some friends and family, and a preorder link to the next book in the back of Second Chance Ranch.

I posted on social media, emailed some friends, and pulled in $196 in 2 weeks.

Now, since I made $1500 for the duration of 2015 on my self-publishing, $196 in a couple of weeks was a major achievement.

This is also when I learned that Book 1 is not always your best-seller. At least not initially. That new shiny thing you love and have poured your heart into? It's invisible. And that's okay. You don't have to come roaring out of the gate. There is always room and time to build and grow. Be patient. Be smart. Work smarter, not harder. Your success will come!

October 2015: I didn't have another book out until December 1. So I have two months here with no releases. That's okay. In October, I started learning about newsletters, though I still didn't set one up.

I started populating my website, ordering covers, and writing more books.

Second Chance Ranch made $111 this month.

November 2015: Again, no new releases here. But Second Chance Ranch had now made 1/4 of my total income for 2015, and I was *thrilled*.

I'd been frequenting Facebook more and more, reading as much as I could, and learning. That's the best and biggest thing I still do for my career. I lurk more than I post. I listen more than I talk. I experiment more than I judge.

In November, I heard about these newsletter service things. BookBub came up. And Robin Reads.

I decided to put together a promotion on Second Chance Ranch for the release of Third Time's the Charm on December 1.

I booked a lot of free or low-priced ads. I applied for a BookBub featured deal and didn't get it.

I did, however, get a Robin Reads feature, and everything was hinging on that....

In November, Second Chance Ranch had a free promo on the 30th. I gave away 1581 copies. The book made $680.

December 2015: Book 2, Third Time's the Charm, released on December 1.

I set Book 1 to free for five days, from November 30 – December 4.

I had a Robin Reads ad on November 30. I had a bunch of piddly other ads the rest of the week. I announced on social media. That's all I had at the time. I still didn't have a newsletter.

I gave away 4500 copies for free over the course of the 5 days.

In December, once the book went back to $3.99, it made $595.

Third Time's the Charm, Book 2, made $637.

This was my first-ever four-figure month in Indie Publishing. I had 2 books out.

The series from September – December, with just 2 books, made: $2219.

I was still thrilled. I had never made this much money with Indie publishing before.

. . .

January 2016: No releases this month. Book 3 is slated for a February 16 release, and in anticipation of...something (haha!), I applied for a BookBub featured deal.

And I got one. I was terrified. It was a lot of money I didn't really have. I'd only been paid for my September royalties at this point, and those weren't even $200.

But I paid for the BookBub featured deal, and I prayed. LOL.

I gave away about 30,000 copies of Book 1.

With Book 1 and Book 2 and the BookBub, I made $5488 in January.

My preorders soared for Book 3.

I started building my newsletter list here as well. I only had links in the front and backs of my published books.

February 2016: Book 3, Fourth and Long, releases on February 16.

I'd been busy writing for future releases, as I only had the first two books written when I started this crazy journey back in September. So I'm writing, writing, writing, in between all of the releasing, planning for sales, and other stuff.

Fourth and Long had a very high number of preorders, most likely from the BookBub the month before, as people read the first two books and had time to preorder the third.

It also had multiple Amazon bestseller flags for the longest period of time (17 days) before it fell at all.

And I know why, though sometimes it's hard to tell. There are a lot of unknowns in publishing sometimes.

But I happened to strike the luckiness quotient, and I had another BookBub featured deal ON release day of Book 3.

Book 2 was free.

I gave away 38,000 copies.

Book 1 and Book 2 made $4160 in February.

Book 3 made $4698.

Combined, the series made $8858.

Almost five figures!

As you can imagine, I was stunned. I'd been in the traditional market for so long, and I couldn't fathom making this kind of money. Of course, at this point in time, I had yet to be paid any of my larger sums, but that was okay.

I could now *see* it.

And I was hooked.

I wanted to write faster. Put out more books. Learn better marketing strategies. Anything I could, because making money doing something I loved was intoxicating.

March 2016: No books releasing this month, but I ran a "Western Weekend Sale" where I put Book 1 at 99¢, made

Book 2 free, and put Book 3 at 99¢. I did this, because I could see my sales were falling.

You can see it too. In March, with the 3 books, I made $4367.

That's less than half of the month before. Is all lost?

Nope.

There are ups and downs in publishing. Now, would I rather be going up every month? Sure. But I was still new. I was still building. I only had three books out, and honestly, my fanbase had probably read through them all last month.

So I hunkered down. I wrote more books. I planned more releases. I stayed the course.

Remember, there was no Amazon Marketing Services for KDP self-published authors at this time. Or, if there was, I didn't know about them. I wasn't using any other ads besides my own newsletter, which I was still building, and the occasional Robin Reads or BookBub-type advertising.

April 2016: Book 4, Fifth Generation Cowboy, hits shelves on April 19.

I was lucky enough to once again get a BookBub featured deal for Book 3 at 99¢. This ran on April 17, leading up to the release of Book 4.

This was the kind of advertising there was. I was doing the best I could. My reader magnet would be out in May, though, and I was actively building my newsletter at this time as well.

This is when instaFreebie exploded onto the scene, as well as other massive newsletter subscriber builders. I did them all. I grew my organic list, which was about 3000 from January – March to 30,000 by October of 2016.

So there's work being done for future sales behind-the-scenes.

Books 1 – 3 made $4980 in April.

Book 4 made $3349 in April.

And I released a boxed set of Books 1 – 3 as well. It made $146 in April.

This was still a few hundred dollars short of a five-figure month. Not there yet.

May 2016: No new releases in this month. I did do a promotion on my Boxed Set, trying to keep the income up.

Total earned, Three Rivers Ranch Romance series: $5195.

June 2016: No new releases this month, and in fact, I did nothing. No marketing. The income reflects this.

I did this, because Book 5 is getting ready to drop in July, and I'm putting everything I have into that release, which is on July 5, 2016.

Total earned, Three Rivers Ranch Romance series: $2890.

This might be depressing. I actually remember thinking, "Wow, that month sucked."

BUT – can you see the tiered launching strategy here? I hit things hard in January, February, and April. I couldn't keep doing it in May and June. Something had to give.

I distinctly remember putting up Book 5 to release on July 5, and I hadn't written a word of it. I had to write the first chapter of the book to go in the final copy of Book 4, and I wrote it and released Book 4.

That means I had less than 11 weeks to get Book 5 written, edited, and packaged. And ready to launch with major marketing.

It was a harrowing time for me, and I vowed I'd never do it again. I bet you know how that turned out...ha! But I didn't do that again for a while actually. I didn't put up another book on preorder I hadn't at least drafted until 2018. So I learned a lesson there too.

After all, I had a demanding day job, church calling, and little children. What if I couldn't get my book ready in time?

So I didn't do that again...for a while.

July 2016: Book 5, The Seventh Sergeant, releases.

I ran a massively huge campaign for the release of this book. I had a decent newsletter following at this time, and

I segmented my newsletter into two parts. There were still no swaps, and no AMS ads.

I did, however, put up my very first Facebook ad for this campaign. It did not go well, as you can imagine, and it would be many more months before I came back to Facebook ads at all. (Advertising platforms take a lot of time, money, and energy to learn how to use. It's worthwhile, but I'd do it on backlist books you already have out, so you can utilize your skills for a Rapid Release strategy.)

I let Book 5 launch, and I held on. Because I'd been lucky enough to get another BookBub featured deal, but it wasn't until July 11.

It was on Book 4.

I put all four books at free.

That's right. Book 1 = free. Book 2 = free. Book 3 = free. Book 4 = free.

The only full priced book I had was the new release.

It was terrifying. But I had faith that free worked. I'd seen it work in the past. I'd done it on a smaller scale.

So I went for it.

Books 1 – 4, and the boxed set made $6393 in July, even with them being free for a few days.

Book 5 made $3910.

I'd also had my reader magnet out for a couple of months at this point, and I put it up for sale on July 15. So I now suddenly had 6 books in this series for sale. This eventually became Book 5, and I moved Book 5 to Book 6 in the order.

In July, this book made $321. <<This lower number makes sense. It's been a reader magnet for a couple of months. Most of my core fans already have this book, so they don't need to buy it.

Make sense?

And, if you've been keeping track of the maths, July 2016—9 months into my Rapid Release every 11 weeks, with 5 books out—I finally made 5-figures.

So does free work?

Free does work. It builds a big, wide, massive fanbase...that wants free books. I didn't know this at the time, though I do now. If I'd started as I meant to go, I might not have done free. But the fact is, free books *can* expand your readership, and *sometimes* that readership will pay for books too. Or borrow in Kindle Unlimited, as some view that as "free."

Needless to say, I spent two years giving away free books. Over and over and over. It wasn't until 2018, when I declared, "No more free books!" and I stopped doing that.

But for a new author, with only a few books, and trying to build...free worked. I think free still works, but if you're not convinced, the best part about Indie publishing is the experimentation.

Try it for yourself and see.

Onward!

. . .

August 2016: No book releasing this month, thank the stars. School starts in August, and it's a very busy time of year for me.

Total made while I went back to school: $4500.

Note: I made roughly half that monthly from my teaching salary.

So for doing nothing but having books out and sending weekly newsletters, I thought I was doing pretty dang good.

September 2016: Book 7, Eight Second Ride, came out on September 20.

I've got no other promotions. I hit July hard. I let this book come out with its preorders and I moved on. After all, September is a pretty busy month too.

Book 1 – 6 made: $3752.

Book 7 made: $2641.

October 2016: No new releases this month. I do have a BookBub featured deal on Book 2 (again). It didn't do very well, because it was a repeat book.

The series made: $6536. Notice that this is up significantly since June and August, both months where not a whole lot happened. Simply having out more books helps.

Now, because I had a release on November 1, all the

preorders dropped on October 31, and I was actually paid for them in October's check instead of November's.

So Christmas in Three Rivers was a compilation of 4 novellas, and I released it at a higher price point than normal.

It made $1300 on October 31.

I also released a second boxed set of Books 4 – 7 in October, and it made $400.

So the series total, of all the books, collections, and boxed sets for October was: $8236. Not bad for no real marketing and no real releases.

November 2016: Book 8, Christmas in Three Rivers launches on November 1. But again, most of the preorders dropped in October, and I didn't do a whole lot for marketing this month.

The series made: $5577 with me just letting the books do their thing. Again, no ads going, as that wasn't really a focus at this time. At least in my world.

December 2016: Book 9, The First Lady of Three Rivers Ranch comes out on December 5. It had a 99¢ preorder, and I was gearing up for a big launch for this final book in the series.

I wasn't even planning to write this book, but I had many fans emailing me, asking for Squire's parents' story.

That's what this book became. It could really be Book 1. It's definitely a second entry point into my series, and I've used it to market as such.

It had a full 90-day preorder, in KU.

It had, by far and away, more preorders than any of the other books.

It only made $1574 in December.

This is when I learned that 99¢ is great for moving bigger quantities of books, but it's not how I'm going to make money.

I've seen and read and heard a lot of people launching their books at 99¢. They say they "seem to" make more money.

My numbers don't lie. It's easy to go back and look at every book in this series and see how much money they made in their launch month. And some of them weren't even released until the latter end of the month.

Look at Eight Second Ride, released on September 20. It made $2641 in 10 days.

First Lady released on December 5. In 21 days, it only made $1574. The lower price point is the only difference.

Maybe they're moving more copies than I am. I don't know. I just know it's a heckuva lot of copies to make up when you're launching at $3.99 compared to 99¢.

Books 1 – 8 (including Christmas and the 2 boxed sets) made $7512

Book 9 made $1574, for a total of $9086.

. . .

We could stop right there, but the fact is, over the course of the next 2+ years, I continue to use those books to build my fanbase, expanding it one reader at a time with low-risk entry points.

But if we do stop right there, I released 9 books, one of which was a 4-novella collection over the course of 16 months. I released 2 boxed sets of those books.

All of these books were in KU. I ran multiple free book promotions on them, built my newsletter list, and continued to work my day job and raise my family.

At the end of that 16 months, I'd made $81,908 on the Three Rivers Ranch Romance series.

It was an excellent Rapid Release strategy for me that allowed me to put out books consistently. Learn how to market them. Learn how to package them. Learn how I worked. Learn what I liked and didn't like.

And that was the beginning of my Indie career. Combined with my traditional deals and royalties, 2016 was the first year I was a six-figure author, and 80% of that was because of Liz Isaacson and Three Rivers Ranch, releasing every 11 weeks.

Recap:

1. What did you see here that you could try?
2. Ask yourself: Have I tried building a readership

with free books? Why wouldn't I want to do this for me personally?

3. Can you write and release a book every quarter?

4. In your mind, what advantages does this Rapid Release strategy have?

5. What more could you do now that there are ad platforms to use? How do you feel about learning those ad platforms? How much do you have to spend on them?

6. What pricing strategy makes the most sense to you?

7. What do you think about preorders?

These are all things to consider when you're contemplating self-publishing. The best part about this career is your ability to try different things for yourself. You don't have to believe me or anyone else you see posting on Facebook or any other forum. You can try it yourself, look at the data, and make business decisions with numbers, not rumors.

Notes and Things To Try:

11

RAPID RELEASING EVERY 6 WEEKS - CASE STUDY 2

Onto the next case study! For this one, we're going to look at 8 months of data, starting with Book 1 in the Gold Valley Romance series by Liz Isaacson, and ending with Book 6 in that same series. (The series has more books now, but the last 2 came later, and weren't part of this Rapid Release strategy.)

The time line goes from January – August 2017. During this time, my pen name of Liz Isaacson released a new book in the Gold Valley Romance series every 6 weeks.

All of the books were released at full price, except for Book 4, which released at 99¢. Full price for this series was $3.99.

All of the books had full 12-week preorders on Amazon.

None of these books were in Kindle Unlimited. I

released these books to a wide audience, on Amazon, but also on Nook, Kobo, iBooks, and Google Play.

And now, my favorite part...the data!

January 2017: Book 1, Before the Leap releases on January 9. This is a spin-off series from my Three Rivers Ranch series. In fact, all of my series spin-off from another one.

In this case, Book 1 here was the brother of the hero in Book 4 in Three Rivers. Just something to note. I used the Three Rivers series to promote this one, but these books were wide, so the options were a bit limited.

I spent a lot of time researching publishing wide, and I'd heard it can take a year—and some luck on BookBub —to find a readership.

This was 2017.

It's 2019 now, and I think that's changed again. The chatter I see is up to 3 years to find a wide audience, and you need a lot more than BookBub.

But in 2017, I determined I'd give it a try for a year, and I'd try booking ads such as BookBub as much as possible. Seriously, that was my strategy. Release often. Pray for BookBub.

At this point, for this series, I am relying solely on my own newsletter once again. My social media. My other books. There wasn't the rush for newsletter swaps you see now. I was still afraid of Facebook ads and the Amazon Ad platform. I dabbled, never satisfied and never sure how things were working.

So keep that in mind. Today's marketplace might be very different if I had the ad knowledge, nerves of steel, and marketing tactics we see in the current IPC. (In fact, I know it is. My later case studies show it.) But I've been around long enough to watch that climate change, grow, morph, and then reinvent itself time and time again.

You might be able to find a strategy here that you haven't thought of. After all, the climate in Indie publishing can shift at any time, possibly even before I get this book edited and published!

Before the Leap made:

Amazon: $1116.09

B&N: $9.48

iTunes: $14.70

Google Play: $7.54

Total sales for Kobo, from January 9 – November 11, 2017, when I put the book in Kindle Unlimited: $22.79. **I grouped all the Kobo income together for each book as it came out, because Kobo was such a poor seller. I made less than $120 there for all 6 books over the course of the timeframe for this case study. Yes, I had their Promotions tab. I ran 5 of them. Less than $120. Kobo was not a good retailer for me.

.   .   .

February 2017: Book 2, After the Fall releases on February 13. This was Book 2, and I hadn't perfected the Tiered Launch Strategy I've talked about previously. I simply let this book come out, and I sent to my newsletter.

Now, you might not be terribly impressed with this. I mean, shouldn't you push every book? I don't think so, and I think every book published is adding to your backlist, and you can choose when to market those books.

I recently rebranded this series. I retitled the books and recovered them. I did another big "launch" on them in February 2019, and the series continues to bring in money, readers, and now, pagereads.

After the Fall made:

Amazon: $804.70

B&N: $4.74

iTunes: $28.94

Google Play: $2.53

Total sales for Kobo, from February 13 – November 11, 2017, when I put the book in Kindle Unlimited: $32.94

Before the Leap made:

Amazon: $445.52

B&N: $4.74

iTunes: $16.66

Google Play: $29.16

March 2017: No releases this month. I didn't do any promotions this month, either. The reason was because I had applied for a BookBub to coincide with the release of Book 3. It took a lot of time and brainpower to set up all the ads I did for the sale, which was a strategy at the time called stacking ads.

This practice is still common, and it can still be effective. Different newsletters do better than others, and at this current time, the only three I'm confident in and using are BookBub, Robin Reads, and Bargain/Free Booksy.

You can find a list of the best ones in this market right now here, at least according to some. Your mileage may vary, as I've seen declining results with ENT for the past several promotions I've used them for. I don't use them anymore.

In March the series made:
Amazon: $829.36
B&N: $23.70
iTunes: $4.80
Google Play: $34.31

. . .

At this point, I'm a little disappointed. Things aren't going as well as I'd hoped. This series that spun off from my fairly successful first series didn't seem to be doing much. But I'm not in despair. I know by now that there are ups and downs and swells and curves in publishing.

And I have a HUGE promotion coming up. So I'm holding my breath for April.

April 2017: Book 3, Through the Mist releases on April 3.

In April, I felt like I'd hit the jackpot. I got a BookBub featured deal on the first book in this series! This was what everyone had told me to do to build a wide audience. Put the books out there, and then try for BookBub. After all, there are a lot of readers on the BB lists.

I was thrilled. Book 1 would be 99¢ on April 8, right after the release of Book 3, and all I could remember was how well my Three Rivers Ranch series had taken off after I had a free Book 1 in that series.

This wasn't free, but I reasoned that 99¢ was a screaming deal for a book. I had 2 more available, and 2 more on preorder.

This was going to go great.

At this time, the Indie community was clamoring for credentials. Everyone and their husband's mother was making a run at the USA Today list.

With this BookBub, I figured I'd give it a shot too. I set

up dozens and dozens of ads, across multiple days, starting BEFORE the BB ad, as it was on a Saturday.

TIP: If you get approved for a BB featured deal and you don't like the date, ask them to move it. They will, if they can. I should've done this. I didn't know then what I know now.

Anyway, I started the book at 99¢ for Monday, April 3 – Sunday, April 9. That's the window for USA Today sales. Monday – Sunday of a week.

I'll detail all the ads I bought for it, but honestly hardly any of these are worth it. But I'll break it down for you, if you're interested.

APRIL 3: KND with BG slideover – paid $120

    Red Roses Romance – paid $10

    eBook of the Day for Nook and iBooks – paid $15

    Read Cheaply – paid $35

    LKBB – paid $5

Sales on April 3:

    33 – Nook

    37 – iBooks

    466 – Amazon

. . .

APRIL 4: Robin Reads – paid $60
  ENT – paid $55
  Love Books (Love, Lust, Lipstick stains) – paid $25

Sales on April 4:
  24 – Nook (total: 57)
  12 – iBooks (total: 49)
  321 – Amazon

Now, you need 500 total sales from either Nook or iBooks to even be considered for the list. I wasn't even getting close. But my BB featured deal hadn't run yet. I was SURE it would be fine by Saturday....

APRIL 5: Started some BookBub ads. More on this later.
  Just Kindle Books – paid $20
  Book Sends credit ($60)
  Many Books – paid $29
  Genre Pulse – paid $14.25
  Reading Deals – free

Sales on April 5:
  42 – Nook (total: 99)

9 – iBooks (total: 58)

155 – Amazon (total: 942)

APRIL 6: Bargain Booksy/Freebooksy – paid $135

Betty Book Freak – paid $18

LJMarsh - Christian Book – paid $16

Hosanna Highest – paid $25

Sales on April 6:

46 – Nook (total: 145)

24 – iBooks (total: 82)

237 – Amazon (total: 1197)

APRIL 7: Price Dropped Books – paid $17

Sales on April 7:

37 – Nook (total: 182)

5 – iBooks (total: 87)

174 – Amazon (total: 1371)

1 – Kobo US (1)

11 – Google Play (11)

APRIL 8: BB deal – paid $420

Sales on April 8:

165 – Nook (total: 347)

112 – iBooks (total: 199)

981 – Amazon (total: 2352)

3 – Kobo US (4)

11 – Google Play (11)

TOTAL: 2804

Sales on April 9:

82 – Nook (total: 429)

37 – iBooks (total: 236)

335 – Amazon (total: 2687)

1 – Kobo US (4)

27 – Google Play (38)

TOTAL: 3394 = $1187.90 earned on Book 1

TOTAL AD SPEND:

$988 on paid advertising

BB ads: $90

Facebook Ads: $500

Total spend: $1578

Sell-through to Book 2 and 3, both at full price at $3.99:

Book 2: 112 = $302.40

Book 3: 83 = $224.10

Pre-orders on Book 4 (99¢): 198 = $69.30

Book 5 ($3.99): 69 = $186.30

With Book 1 earnings from the promo, I made $1970 that week on the 3 books that were out, and the preorders of the other 2 books. I spent $1578 to do it.

NOTE: BookBub ads were VERY new at this time. I had no idea what I was doing. The same was true for Facebook ads. I didn't know how to use them. In fact, it wasn't until years later that I dug into those paid advertising platforms and really figured them out.

And I see I set up 20 NL swaps for this week too. I think this was the very first time I'd ever done them.

So this was the type of promotions that were happening at this time in 2017. I still think these type of paid newsletter promotions can be valuable, but you need to be selective about which ones you choose. And remember, you can't be constantly putting your books at free and 99¢ either. You'll see more of this in a case study coming up.

My personal philosophy is this: If a book is free, you can't really use it again to promote for 6 months. 99¢ is three months.

There are always more readers out there. Just because you've had promotions or sales doesn't mean you're tapped out. It just means you need to be more strategic in your promotions and marketing.

The series made in April:

Amazon: $3891.89 ($1365.41 of this is from Book 3.)
B&N: $484.66
iTunes: $250.01
Google Play: $92.07

Finally! I thought. The series had made some real money, and not just on Amazon. Book 3 had some decent preorders too, and combined with this sale, it made $1365 this month by itself.

Let's see how the 99¢ release compares! I've got people into the series now. At least I hoped I had. I'd moved thousands of copies of Book 1, and it had good reviews. I was hopeful.

I should note here also, that in April, I moved my books from Draft2Digital, a distributor I was using to distribute the books to Nook and iBooks, to direct-selling on Nook and iBooks, through Nook Press and the iTunes Connect platforms.

I did this because at this time, I came in contact with both an Apple rep and a B&N rep, but they could only help me if I was selling directly from their platforms. They're not hard to set up and use, but D2D was easier and everything was centralized.

But I can't move Book 4 until it releases, as I had preorders I didn't want to mess up. But by the end of May, all the books were on the direct sites to sell.

. . .

May 2017: Book 4, Between the Reins releases on May 16. This was a 99¢ release. The idea was that I'd already gotten Book 1 on a BookBub featured deal while this book was on preorder. I didn't hit the USA Today bestseller list with that BookBub, and I thought, well, maybe I should try with a new release.

After all, Book 1 had been out for 2 months before I really pushed it, and I'd sold a lot of copies already. But what would a new release at 99¢ do?

I also wanted to test again the theory behind releasing at 99¢. There were, and still are, many people using this strategy, and I wanted to see if I'd make the same amount of money with this strategy simply by moving more copies.

Keep in mind, you have to move almost 8 times the volume at 99¢ that you do at $3.99 to make the same amount of money. Depending on your goals, one pricing strategy might win out over the other.

I've always wanted to make money. I've never cared about rank or freaked out about visibility. This has changed in the recent past, but in 2017, I wasn't concerned with Top 1000 or Top 100.

Honestly, I was happier. I was making money, and writing books I loved, and promoting them the best way I knew how. Now, when I release a book, I'm almost a basket case, constantly checking rank to see how I'm doing.

That's fine if that's what you're using as a measuring stick. But I want to run my business smarter, with data, so I can have concrete evidence *for myself* for what works for my genre, my books.

At this time, moving more copies meant more readers, in my mind. And more readers means more money down the line. I'm willing to wait for my money, if I need to. That's why I gave away so many free books. Get a fan in through a low-risk funnel (free or 99¢), and you could potentially make thousands off that person as they read your future books when they come out.

Let's see what happened with this 99¢ release.

Between the Reins made:

Amazon: $623.51. It sold 1657 copies at 99¢. That's a lot more than my usual preorders and sales for a release month. But it's not almost 8 times more. And $623 is MUCH less than Book 3 in its first month out. In fact, it was HALF as much.

B&N: $30.09

iTunes: $24.66

Google Play: $5.92

Total sales for Kobo, from May 16 – November 11, 2017, when I put the book in Kindle Unlimited: $26.80

. . .

The series made in May:

Amazon: $1694.42

B&N: $49.24

iTunes: $42.83

Google Play: $26.52

Aaaand, I was disappointed. The series had made less than half of April, and the numbers at the non-Zon retailers? In the toilet. The readers had not come over yet, and I was starting to doubt if they would at all. The tail for BookBub wasn't nearly as long as it had been for my KU books, and it seemed as if readers hadn't made it through the series to Book 4 yet.

Which is fine. I've said that I'm willing to wait for readers to read, and I reminded myself that sometimes people won't read a free book for 6 months. If ever.

Meanwhile, I started toying with the idea of moving the books to Kindle Unlimited once the last one was out. After all, I was five months in now, and I'd had the coveted BookBub, and it didn't seem to have captured any readers on non-Zon platforms.

But I'd already written the books, and they were up for preorder, and I was going to soldier on.

By the way, this book is not a debate about whether wide or Kindle Unlimited is better. I'm simply reporting my own findings and what I thought about them, as well as how I used the data to make my business decisions on this Rapid Release strategy.

June 2017: Book 5, Over the Moon releases on June 26. This is a very-end-of-the-month release, so I spent most of the month writing and getting ready for release. I spent a lot of time building my newsletter and getting the automation set for it during the summer months.

I didn't set up any special promotions. I focused on connecting with my readers, emailing every Tuesday, and expanding my fanbase. It's important that authors have this infrastructure, as you shouldn't have to, and probably won't do as well, if you're relying on someone else to send out the news of your new release.

Amazon is spotty as to when they'll send a new release email. BookBub will, but again, only to your followers. Utilizing Facebook audiences of people who have inter-acted with your posts or website is invaluable.

But you need a Facebook page for that. A website. And the Facebook pixel set up on your website to start collecting that data. This book is not about any of that, and it's a rabbit hole we can fall down for hours.

We don't have hours in this case study, but you can Google and find tons of information about the Facebook pixel and how to install it on your site. It's pretty easy. Make sure you read up on the GDPR as well, as if you're collecting data from the people visiting your website, they should get to know that. You need a privacy policy on your site, and it's also pretty easy to do.

Phew. I'm out of the rabbit hole! My point here is, yes, there are a lot of tasks on the business management side of being an author. It's called infrastructure, and it's worth your time and energy to set it up. If you haven't started that yet, you should, as the larger your infrastructure is, the less you have to rely on anyone but yourself to sell books.

That said, let's look at the numbers for June.

Over the Moon made:

Amazon: $1283.35 <<Again, this is TWICE what Book 4 made at 99¢, and this book didn't even come out until June 26. In only 4 days of sales, it outsold Book 4 at 99¢, which had half a month to sell.

So, I learned that a 99¢ launch price didn't make me more money, and I resolved to stay the course with my $3.99 launch pricing.

B&N: $7.77

iTunes: $18.60

Google Play: $2.59

Total sales for Kobo, from June 26 – November 11, 2017, when I put the book in Kindle Unlimited: $27.93.

. . .

The series made in June:
  Amazon: $2088.88
  B&N: $32.39
  iTunes: $34.83
  Google Play: $3.21

And once again, I'm seeing no traction on non-Zon retailers. I don't want to throw in the towel too early, but I'm frustrated. I've been applying to BookBub, and I get one in July for a free Book 3. Let's see how that did.

July 2017: No releases (except for a different series. I mean, who's crazy? *I'm* crazy! Read the next case study to see how this summer went. Short answer: Crazy.)

I was lucky enough to get another BookBub on this series. Book 3 was picked up in the Christian Fiction category, worldwide, all retailers, for free.

Finally! I thought. *I'm going to hit on the wide audiences*, I told myself. *This is what everyone had told me to do*, I assured myself and anyone who would listen to me. After all, the series has been plugging along, but it's not doing great, in all honesty. I can see it's not, but I'm not sure what to do about it.

I needed to put in a year, right?

Really *try*, right?

So I was thrilled to get this BookBub featured deal. The last one was for 99¢, and I was sure this free one would bring the readers on Apple, B&N, and the other retailers in droves.

On Amazon alone, I gave away 35,000 copies. 4200 on Nook. 4300 on iBooks. Only 200 on Google Play. And Kobo has always been negligible, and I simply report on that as a whole for the 11 months the series was available there.

That's a lot of free copies. I was thrilled. I mean, if I could get even 10% of those people to BUY another book, that would be better than the $30 paydays I was seeing at Nook and iTunes, which admittedly were the ones I cared about.

The series made in July:
Amazon: $2223.76
B&N: $264.18
iTunes: $358.38
Google Play: $439.00

August 2017: Book 6, Under the Bridge releases on August 7. I didn't have anything special planned for this release. I'd just run the free BookBub in July, and this was Book 6. My attention was divided by the summer series, and going back to school, and I just let this book come out.

Under the Bridge made:
  Amazon: $1558.58
  B&N: $59.57
  iTunes: $52.02
  Google Play: $34.31
  Total sales for Kobo, from August 7 – November 11, 2017, when I put the book in Kindle Unlimited: $22.34.

The series made in August:
  Amazon: $2586.20
  B&N: $181.30
  iTunes: $213.09
  Google Play: $218.32

Total series income from January – August:
  Amazon: $15,680.82
  B&N: $1054.43
  iTunes: $964.24
  Google Play: $852.66
  Kobo: $143.97

. . .

Total non-Zon retailers: $2145.30

Total Amazon: $15,680.82

Based on this data, I moved all 6 of these books in Kindle Unlimited on November 11, 2017. I made more in the first 35 days the books were in KU page reads than I did in the 11 months they were wide.

For me, the numbers didn't lie.

I make more money in Kindle Unlimited. So that's where I am now. For me, KU is an all-in or all-out philosophy. Of course, your experience might be different. You might know other authors who have some series in KU and some out and do great. Remember, your mileage may vary with regards to everything I say.

For me, my numbers indicate I make more in KU, so that's where I am. At the time of this writing, KU pagereads account for approximately 65% of my income.

Recap:

1. What did you see here that you could try?
2. Ask yourself: Have I tried building a readership with other platforms? Why wouldn't I want to do this for me personally?
3. Can you write, edit, package, and release a book every 6 weeks on MULTIPLE platforms?

4. In your mind, what advantages does this Rapid Release strategy have?
5. Have you ever tried launching books wide, on more platforms than Amazon? Why or why not?

Notes and Things To Try:

12

RAPID RELEASING EVERY 3 WEEKS - CASE STUDY 3

Oh, this case study. *shakes head* I learned a lot with this Rapid Release strategy, including that one should not start a second series when they're still releasing a previous one—especially if they're still semi-new and don't have a huge fanbase. Like, Jupiter huge.

For this series, which is the Brush Creek Brides series, I released a new book every three weeks, starting in June 2017 and going through September 2017.

If you read the last case study, you saw that I didn't finish my second series until August 2017, and this one was well on by then.

Mistake.

I would not do this again. My attention was split, and my audience was not nearly big enough to handle so many books coming at them all the time.

So I learned that, and I'm not going to say I never did

this again.... But at least I learned something that I do *try* to use now. Haha.

There were 6 books in this series, and they were priced at $2.99. I marketed them as "evening reads," and they were all short, 30,000-word novellas. My tagline was "3 bucks. 2 hours to read. 1 satisfying romance."

I was marketing these as summer reading, kind of like how USA has summer series on during the slower TV-watching months of the year. (Hello, *Suits!* One of my favorite shows.) I took that idea and combined it with James Patterson's "Bookshots," which were being marketed as shorter novels, "no filler," and under $5.

So let's look at this data.

June 2017: Book 1, A Wedding for the Widower, came out on June 13. This book had a full 90-day preorder, as did all the books in this series. They all launched at $2.99.

Book 1 made $925.63 in June. It had 251 preorders. At this stage of my career, I was using preorders to judge the success of a series. Now, it didn't really influence whether I would write more books or not, because in a Rapid Release Launch, all the books were already written. I was about 6-7 months ahead in my production schedule at this time, so all 6 books were already done.

That said, I do watch my preorders, even today. I want at least 1 more from book to book. This tells me people are reading and enjoying the books as they come out.

Now, a word of caution here. If you do Rapid Releasing, which is what this book is about, sometimes you don't have the time you need to use the preorders as a judge for whether a series is valuable and worth your time or not.

So it's not failsafe. Nothing is, right?

But it is something I'm going to note in this series.

July 2017: Book 2, A Companion for the Cowboy, came out on July 4. It had 198 preorders Book 3, A Bride for the Bronc Rider, came out on July 25. It has 232 preorders.

You'll note that neither one of those is as high as Book 1.

I know why, and it's a valuable lesson I learned about my readers and my genre. Book 2 is a romance with an older cowboy in his thirties, and a millennial heroine.

Oh, boy. My readers—most of whom are grand-mothers—did not like that heroine. I learned quickly that I needed to stick to the thirties for my romances, especially for the heroines. Not only that, but I used this data to create an entire series of 40+ heroines that is hugely popular.

So even "mistakes" can give you valuable information.

But that's Book 2. So it did not do as well, and it still does not sell as well as some of the other books in the series. I suppose I could go back and rewrite it, but her age is such a huge part of her growth that it would be like writing a whole new book. So I haven't done that, nor do I plan to do that. But it is a lesson I learned.

But from Book 2 to Book 3, the preorders were up again. This could've been a summer thing. Book 2 came out on the Fourth of July, a popular holiday in the US. There are a variety of things that could've happened.

I did not do any promotional pricing on Book 1 for the releases of Book 2 or 3. I relied on my newsletter and got the books out.

Companion made: $917.20

Bride made: $608.06

Series made: $1895.53

August 2017: Book 4, A Family for the Farmer, came out on August 15. It had 237 preorders. More than Book 3! Yay!

Family made: $1001.95

Series made: $2147.27

September 2017: Book 5, A Home for the Horseman, came out on September 5. It had 235 preorders. Not as many as Book 4, but it was only down by 2. I'm calling that a win when it's back-to-school season.

. . .

Book 6, A Refuge for the Rancher, came out on September 26. It had 290 preorders. The highest of them all! People were liking the series. Phew.

Home made: $1189.23

Refuge made: $950.78

Series made: $3831.05

So for the summer, four months from June – September, these 6 books made $8799.48.

I was happy with that. I didn't do any promotional pricing on ANY of the books. Every book dropped at $2.99 and stayed there. Because BookBub requires a book to be 150 pages, none of these books qualified for their featured deal.

So at the end of August, I did bundle together Book 1 and Book 2 and I submitted the duo to BookBub. That ran on September 14, and that duo made $1372.16 in September and October from that feature.

So this Rapid Release didn't get a lot of marketing. At the time, shorter romances weren't a big thing. Did I make tons of money from this?

It appears not.

BUT – that doesn't mean it was a fail. I went on to add 6 more books to the series the next year, and I'm continually adding new readers to my backlist and catalog with low-risk entry points into the series and low-spend ads.

Just one reader earns me 15,000 pages if they read all

the books. I've said this before, but it bears repeating: Books do NOT need to make all of their money in the first week or month or even year of their life. The digital bookshelf has limitless space, and there are limitless opportunities to get new readers into your backlist.

Now, if you think you've written a really terrible book, by all means, take it down. Or if it doesn't fit your brand, as I'll be talking about that in a future case study. But just because a book or a series isn't gangbusters on the bank account doesn't mean it wasn't worth doing.

To go out a few more months, I'll put the total income for this series from June – December, 2017. The 6 books and the duo bundle made $13,602.02. And by the time Book 7 hit shelves the next summer, the series was closing in on $20,000.

That's not bad for 6 books, with no marketing, no ads, and no price reductions. Is it as good as some of my other series? Nope, it sure isn't. And that's why there's no Brush Creek Brides books coming out in summer 2019.

Data doesn't lie.

But for the sake of the case study, I published 6 more books in the summer of 2018 (read on for the case study on those, as I published a new book every week!), and the total 12 book series, over 18 months (June 2017 – December 2018) made almost $46,000.

That's an average of $2366.50 per month. And that's STILL more than I made teaching in one month. So just the income from those 12 books alone can replace my monthly teaching salary.

Don't discount your backlist. Don't ignore it either. Yes, this is a book about Rapid Releasing, but do you have a plan for the books once they're a year old? Two years? Think about it. You might need one.

Recap:

1. What did you see here that you could try?
2. Ask yourself: Have I tried building a readership with shorter books? Why wouldn't I want to do this for me personally?
3. Can you write, edit, package, and release a book every three weeks?
4. In your mind, what advantages does this Rapid Release strategy have?
5. What do you see around in other media platforms (movies, TV, Internet streaming) that you could take and implement in your book marketing strategy?

Notes and Things To Try:

13

RAPID RELEASING EVERY WEEK - CASE STUDY 4

I loved writing my shorter romances in the Brush Creek Brides series under Liz Isaacson, and the following summer (2018), I decided to do 6 more books, this time releasing one every week. I did this in June and July 2018, taking off the first week of June and the first week of July.

My longer Three Rivers Ranch series was doing well, and I thought it would be smart to have another long series. I already had 6 Brush Creek Brides, and I like writing shorter novella-type romances, and I'd learned that family sagas were big in romance.

So I created the Fuller family, who had a lot of children—some of them already married—and I wrote 6 new novels for 7 of the siblings. Really? How did you fit in 7 siblings in 6 books?

One of them is a dual romance, told from 4 POVs. The

Partner for the Paramedic was a challenge I gave myself as an author, as writing novel after novel can become quite stale...as I'm sure some of you know.

So I took the Fuller twin sisters and they each got a HEA with paramedic partners in the book. It was fun, and challenging, and I enjoyed writing it!

Here's how things played out with the new books in the series, with a Rapid Release strategy of once/week.

June 2018: Book 1, A Marriage for the Marine, came out on June 12. Book 2, A Fiancé for the Firefighter, came out on June 19. Book 3, A Treasure for the Trooper, came out on June 26. I'm tired just typing all of that.

Now, I had recently learned that I could indeed put a newly released book on a Kindle Countdown Deal as long as it had been on preorder for longer than 30 days. My goal here was to create a Release Day team of readers who could buy at 99¢ or read in KU when I asked them to.

I sent emails for the group. I made a Facebook group. Everything was going great.

As some of you might know, the summer of 2018 was a crazy time in Indie publishing, with KDP specifically. They made the rule about only putting 10% bonus content in the back of a book on June 1, 2018, and "book stuffers" were getting their accounts frozen or disabled left and right.

One practice from one of these authors was "bribing" people to buy the book or read it in KU on a specific day. So...all my plans for a Release Day team? They didn't really work. I didn't want to be seen as bribing people, though I never did. I tried for a couple of the releases, which I'll note below, but I didn't see hardly any success with it, and my Release Day team is now pretty much a defunct group where I post about sales on my books from time to time.

Again, mistakes are made in Indie publishing, right? I don't consider it a mistake. I have never bribed my readers to buy or read on a certain day, nor incentivized reviews. I have never done anything against the KDP Terms of Service, and many authors have street teams and release day teams that are run according to TOS guidelines.

I decided, given the climate, that I didn't want to be anywhere near the appearance of bribing or incentivizing. So I only did special pricing for the first few releases, which I'll tell you about.

Not only that, but who reading this hasn't experienced an Amazon glitch? If you haven't, knock on wood and throw up a prayer of gratitude! I had some really frustrating ones during these launches. Read on to find out about them!

So let's start with Book 1. It came out on June 12 and sure enough, I was able to schedule a Kindle Countdown Deal (KCD) for June 18! I was excited. I made the book 99¢, announced to my Release Day Team, and set the

KCD for 3 days—right over the release day of Book 2, which was the 19th.

Book 2 came out on the 19th at full price, and I was going to set it for a KCD for the following week.

Nope.

Amazon had locked me out for 30 days. I called them, explained everything, and they said, "We don't know why you can't do it. We'll have the technical team look at it."

Now...if you've ever gotten that message from KDP before, you know that means you're looking at at least a week of nothing while they "investigate."

I can't even pretend to know the enormity of issues KDP can have at any given time, but I knew one thing: I wasn't going to be running a KCD on Book 2 as Book 3 launched.

So I had a decision to make. Manually set the price to 99¢? Or leave it at full price?

I had the Release Day team I had *just* started. I'd promised them the books would be in KU or only 99¢.

What to do?

I left the books at full price. I explained to my Release Day team what was happening, and I set the KCDs for July. So Book 2 and Book 3 just came out at full price on their respective release days.

Book 1 made: $1472.49

Book 2 made: $762.66

Book 3 made: $827.67

VERY interesting for me to see that Book 3 once again outsold Book 2. I'm not sure why, though I have my suspicions. It's the cover. I need a new one for Book 2, so I better put that on my list of things to do!

I took a week off—the week of July 4—and I switched from a Tuesday release to a Thursday release for July. Just to test. You know the name of the Indie game...experimentation!

July 2018: Book 4, A Date for the Detective, came out on July 12. Book 5, A Partner for the Paramedic, came out on July 19. Book 6, A Catch for the Chief came out on July 26.

Okay, so here, I decided to do something I swore I wouldn't do in 2018—give away free books. 2018 was the year I decided to stop doing free books through my KDP Select days. In 2017, I'd given away 750,000 free books, and I decided I needed to start training readers to pay full price for my books, read in KU, or wait for 99¢ sales.

Funny how I made triple the money in 2018 that I did in 2017...

Now, you might be going, "But Elana, a couple of chapters ago, you said free works."

I know what I said.

But Liz is not a new author anymore. She has a deep backlist at this point in her career. Your career will have stages too. Newer authors should consider all options until they have the PERSONAL experience and data to make business decisions.

And I made one for my pen name at the beginning of 2018: No more free books.

Kind of.

LOL.

I offered Book 4, A Date for the Detective, to my newsletter subscribers only. I like to give them exclusive deals every once in a while, and this was one of those times.

I offered the book through BookFunnel, for a limited time of 4 days, before the book was for sale on Amazon.

If they didn't open their emails and download, they missed it.

Now, my diehard fans are going to do that. My core fans. The ones who usually buy right away, or preorder. Right?

So you'll see some lower numbers for Book 4. I wasn't worried about it. I'm still not. There are multiple ways to bring people into a new series, and this was one I used for this particular book.

I did have a KCD on Book 2 in July. I ran it from Monday to Saturday, the week of the launch of Book 6.

I also had a KCD on Book 3 from July 5 – 9. This was the "off week" when I wasn't releasing a new book, if you'll recall.

These weren't the only glitches in the KCD program I had this summer. I tried to do sales on my sweet billionaires (case study coming up!) and couldn't. They had the same problem Book 2 did. My call to KDP yielded the same results. I no longer count on doing a KCD for at least 30 days after the launch of a book.

Bummer?

Maybe.

But all is not lost. I rolled with it. I announced to my Release Day team about each release and the 3 KCDs I did manage to do.

Here's the income for July:

Book 4 (remember this is the one I gave away for free to NL subscribers): $1143.77

Book 5: $1232.31

Book 6: $1157.10 – in 5 days.

Surprisingly, Book 6 sells the best out of all of the books released this summer, except for Book 1. I'm not sure why. It's a fairytale retelling, so that might have something to do with it. I personally think the cover is the cutest, so that might have something to do with it too.

Although, my Book 6s almost always sell really well for some reason. Better than Book 4 or 5, though in my head, people should've read those books BEFORE Book 6.

So for the two months of Rapid Release, the series made $12,000 and racked up over 2 million pagereads.

I was happy with it.

A note about ads:

At this time in my career, I am using Amazon Ads almost exclusively. It was about July 2018 that I started experimenting with Facebook ads again, at least past the occasional boosted post. I did ads on Book 1 in this series and Book 6, and they seemed to do really well.

In total, I spent $1961 on Amazon and Facebook ads in June and July to sell this series. Not a bad ROI. Spending $2K to make $12K.

In August, the series made $5164.91. This is all 12 books now, as you'll recall that I had 6 books out the previous summer.

In September, the series made $3466.17, so I could see things starting to taper. That was fine. I let it go, as I have other things hatching and other books to focus on. But there in the background? This series is always simmering.

You see, I've set Book 1 in the series to 99¢ and I'm advertising it with low spends and tested audiences on both Amazon and Facebook. If I can get readers into a 12-book series by offering a low-risk entry point (free or 99¢), for pennies, I'm going to do it.

I never spend more than 20¢ per click on these ads,

and I've seen my audience and fanbase expanding a little more each day.

Again, I'm not advertising every single book I've written and published. Just a select few that I think can hook readers and propel them through my backlist and catalog, which is quite large at this point.

Not there yet?

Don't worry! Take notes, file things away for later. Do your best. Be yourself. Set goals, and work to achieve them.

Recap:

1. What did you see here that you could try?
2. Ask yourself: Have I tried building a readership of whale readers by releasing quickly? Why wouldn't I want to do this for me personally?
3. Can you write, edit, package, and release a book every single week?
4. In your mind, what advantages does this Rapid Release strategy have?
5. What pricing strategies did you see here that you could use?

Notes and Things To Try:

14

DOUBLING DOWN ON RELEASES OR RAPID RELEASING TWO BOOKS ON THE SAME DAY - CASE STUDY 5

Oh, boy, this case study was intense. I had written a few books in a clean billionaire romance series, and the genre had exploded as summer approached. My books were beach romances. I wasn't going to release them until late summer/fall, but with the popularity on the rise, I decided to get them out there quickly.

I released the first two books on the same day.

Then a month later, I released two more books on the same day.

And a month after that, I released the last two books on the same day.

These books were all in Kindle Unlimited. The first four books were released at 99¢, while the last two were listed at $2.99.

The books had very short preorder periods, if they had one at all. I'll note that below.

Here's how things played out—and how data can help you determine pricing strategies. Again, there's no "seem to" or "maybe" here. There's just data. And data drives our business. When the data says a longer preorder and higher price point help me reach my goals, I follow the data.

That can be tough, I know. I've tried so many things, I can't even tell you about everything. I'm swayed by the winds out there too. The loud voices. The authors who seem to have all their ducks in a row and know exactly how to help you line yours up too.

But the truth is, what works for one author might not work for you. As you go through the book, I hope you've kept your own goals in mind and have made notes of what you think might work well for you personally. Your writing style. Your personality. Your budget. Your drive, time, etc.

None of that is going to look exactly like mine. But I've peeled back the layers to sheer transparency so you can see what I've done. Hopefully, it'll spark something in you that will take your career to the next level.

Let's look at the data when I released these 6 books in pairs.

May 2018: Books 1 and 2, The Brainy Billionaire and The Brawny Billionaire release on April 30.

First, let me start by saying these are Elana Johnson books. Now, Elana's been around for a long time. It's my real name. She started in traditional publishing in 2009, with an agent and a book deal from Simon & Schuster for a young adult dystopian novel. Remember how I said they wouldn't buy my next series? How I started self-publishing that backlist of dystopian, science fiction, and fantasy novels?

Well, it took me a while to get all of that down. I had to get rights back. I had to take books down. I had to do an entire rebrand.

While all of that was going on behind the scenes, I was writing adult contemporary romances. I'd actually started doing this in 2015, and I signed with a new agent then, and she sold my first adult sweet contemporary romance to a publisher.

It has been a terrible experience.

If you've been keeping track, Liz started in 2015 too. I didn't know I could make money self-publishing romance at that time.

I know now that I can.

But I didn't then. And we only know what we know when we know it, right?

So if there's something you don't know right now, it's okay. You can keep learning. You can fix things.

So that's what I was doing. "Fixing" things behind the scenes. Writing more and more sweet contemporary romance for adults. And I needed to re-launch Elana into this genre.

All of my old science fiction and fantasy novels are gone now, except for the 4 with Simon & Schuster. They still own the rights these many years later, and my books are still in print—a huge feat in the traditional market. Most books go to pulp and out of print within 2 years, in case you didn't know.

Mine have been out for 8, and they're still in print. I still get paid royalties from them. It's a small check twice a year, but I don't say no to money. LOL.

Anyway, now that you know all of that, we can move on with the case study.

Basically, Elana Johnson was a brand new author. So if that's where you are, you can hopefully learn something from all of this!

Sweet Billionaire Romance:

These books broke from my norm. Number one, there was no preorder period. I put the books up and published them. Live launch, we call this.

Number two, I priced these books at 99¢ upon launch. I was trying some different things, including a strategy I'd heard about called slow launch. The idea was to put the books up, get everything lined up (like claiming the books on Author Central, BookBub, newsletter swaps and the like, etc.) and then "launching" the books that way.

I had no idea what I was doing, and this whole slow launch strategy went against everything I've been doing for the past 3 years. So I struggled with it. I hated the deluge of tasks that had to be done once the books went live—things I usually had 3 months to get in place before launching a book.

But the books were out now! *Now!* I had to get ready.

I was teaching. It was stressful. I didn't like it.

But I did it.

I kept the books at 99¢ for 2 full weeks.

Brainy made: $3023.82, with most of that coming in the form of KU pagereads. I sold 706 copies at 99¢, with an additional 154 at full price of $2.99 once the price went back up.

Brawny made: $1913.96, again a large portion of this income coming from KU pages. Only 386 copies sold at 99¢, and 101 at full price.

I find this data very interesting. I honestly wasn't expecting Book 1 to cannibalize Book 2. They were both 99¢. They were both billionaires – a VERY hot genre at the time (and arguably, still, at the time of writing).

I found it interesting that I sold so many fewer copies at 99¢, but once the price went up, the differential between the sales of Book 1 and Book 2 wasn't nearly as large.

I wasn't sure what to do with this data, honestly. I was thrilled I'd made $5000 in one month on two books, especially as this was a complete rebranding of Elana Johnson's work. She was brand-new to readers.

Two books.

Five thousand dollars.

I thought it was off to a great start!

June 2018: Books 3 and 4, The Bashful Billionaire and the Brawny Billionaire release on May 29.

Determined to try this strategy again, I once again did not release these two books at full price. They were both 99¢, both a live launch. I set up swaps. I bought some ads. I dug in for 2 weeks. Books 1 and 2 were back up to full price, and I left them there.

I left both books at 99¢ for 2 full weeks.

Bashful made: $2833.94, with 368 sales at 99¢, a lot of pagereads, and 183 sales at full price.

Brawny made: $2764.92, with 268 sales at 99¢, a lot of pagereads, and 187 sales at full price.

Again, the bulk of this income came in the form of pagereads. I was learning that this genre had readers in KU. Liz's books did too, but not nearly to this extent.

I found this FASCINATING. I was expecting Book 3 to

cannibalize Book 4 again, the same way Book 1 had canni-balized Book 2 in May. But that didn't really happen. I'm not entirely sure why. My launch strategy for them was the same. I happen to love Book 2's cover, so I wasn't sure if that was it. The title? What didn't people like about it? Or perhaps, since the series was new, people were only buying Book 1 in May to test the waters. After all, Elana hadn't ever published an adult romance before. The Brainy Billionaire was her first. Prior to this time, remember, she'd been publishing YA dystopian, science fiction, fantasy, and some YA contemporary romance novels in verse.

These billionaires were a brand-new foray.

I honestly think that had something to do with why Book 1 outsold Book 2 so much in May. Because when we look at June's numbers for Book 1 and 2, we see:

Brainy made: $1895.50.

Brawny made: $1430.98.

Now, I always expect Book 1 to outsell the rest of the series. It's the one you discount, you run free days on, all of that. It's how you bring people to your body of work. So it has to be good. Well-edited. Packaged well. And strategi-cally marketed.

The series in June earned: $8925.34 with 4 books out.

This summer was the summer I went whole-hog with Amazon Marketing Services ads, now just called Amazon Advertising. It had been around for a while, but I'd spent a year making ads, freaking out when I didn't understand how they worked, and turning them off.

I grew some nerves of steel, and I figured out the advertising platform. I learned how to calculate read-through, something I had been doing for a while anyway, but I hadn't really attributed any of that to advertising yet. I kept the ads going. I experimented until I found keywords that worked for me.

This summer was also when I returned to Facebook ads with great vigor, spurred on by my AMS advertising success. The process was much slower, and I started with Liz Isaacson books, so there's no data to report in this case study about those.

In June, to make my nearly $9000, I spent $1000 on Amazon Ads on this series. I was thrilled with that result, but things are about to change....

July 2018: Books 5 and 6, The Billionaire's Bodyguard and The Billionaire's Boyfriend release on July 4.

I did a 35-day preorder on these 2 books at the full price of $2.99. So they were both available to purchase at full price when Book 3 and Book 4 launched in June.

After that, I dropped the price to 99¢ for the official launch, but I'd decided to do it for a much shorter time-frame. Only 5 days instead of 2 weeks. I made Book 1 free, and the other 3 books in the series 99¢ to generate more interest in these new books, in case I'd missed some readers over the past two months.

I did not see the great success I'd seen in previous launch strategies using this same method in other series. Why? My belief: People had already gotten Books 1 – 4 on a pretty screaming deal. 99¢ is nothing to sneeze at.

So the books weren't a "deal." They were just more 99¢ noise to the pile. The free book got some attention, and I think overall, this strategy helped launch Books 5 and 6, but the income wasn't anything like I'd seen in other series where I reduce the price of previous books to celebrate the launch of later books.

The 99¢ launch removed that option for me. Readers interested in discounted books had likely already gotten the first four books during the launch weeks I had them at that low price.

You basically have three pricing tiers.

1. Full price
2. 99¢ sale price
3. Free

There's nowhere to go after that.

But let's see what the books did for the month:

Book 5: The Billionaire's Bodyguard made: $2969.93, with 267 full-price preorders, 260 sales at 99¢, pagereads, and 136 sales once it was back to $2.99

Book 6: The Billionaire's Boyfriend made: $2654.04, with 161 full-price preorders, 251 sales at 99¢, pagereads, and 126 sales once it was back to $2.99.

Book 1 was free, and I gave away 12,522 copies. Then it made: $1861.14 after it went back to full price.

Book 2 made: $1413.25

Book 3 made: $1723.85

Book 4 made: $1804.51

Now, I definitely think having the two books up for preorder at the same time cost me some preorder sales on Book 6. But overall, it was right there with Book 5 for the month. Also interesting to me, because Book 2 is STILL the lowest earner out of them all.

And the funny thing? It stays that way indefinitely.

Even until today.

I'm not sure why. I honestly don't know. I think the cover is to-brand and to-market. I think the blurb is great. I love the story. I'm not sure why people are skipping that one and moving down the series. It's something I'm still working on figuring out. Isn't Indie publishing fun?!

Anyway, in July, with the 6 books out now, the series made: $12,426.72. I spent $952 in Amazon Ads to do it.

I was ecstatic. Remember how everyone is on their own journey? And there's always going to be someone higher than you and someone lower than you.

You might be looking at these numbers going, Dude, I make that with one book every month. Or you might be looking at the data going, Holy cow, I'd die to make that much with 6 books.

It's all about perspective.

For me, at this time, that much money from 6 books, from a brand-new, re-branded name?

It was a huge success...that nearly killed me. LOL! But launching two books on the same day was not an easy feat, and I'm not sure I'd do it again.

But it was such a success, based on the hot genre, that I decided to write two more books in the series that will come later. Both came out in November. Still beach romances, when November isn't really a beachy month for most of the United States....

Let's look at the numbers for the series as a whole from August to December. I think it's important to look at data as time goes on. Readers need time to read free books, for one. Giving away 12,000 copies was awesome, but I'm well-aware that some readers will NEVER read the book. It just sits on their Kindle.

I know some readers take months to get to books they don't pay for. I'm willing to give them time to get through the books, and I watch the series to see how things are going. Here's an overview:

. . .

August 2018: $4788.53 – a MUCH lower amount than July. Why, do you think? I have theories, and August is the month you'll see posts going up on just about every author Facebook group about sales slumping. The billionaires weren't a focus for me in August—I put my money somewhere else.

September 2018: $2429.30 – wow! Time to call an SOS, right? Nah. I've been around long enough not to freak out with ebbs and flows.

There's a new book coming, and again, I'm focused on other things. You'll get to see what in a case study coming up: the Christmas in Coral Canyon Romance series, which I was releasing starting in August. Money can come from a variety of places, and I think it should ebb and flow. So you don't need to put all of your eggs in the same basket.

You'll go bankrupt, for one.

And you'll go batty, for two.

And who can write under those conditions?

Remember, marketing could be a full-time job. Don't let it be. Be an author. Think smarter. Set goals and outline plans to achieve them. Experiment. Start as you mean to go.

And give yourself—and readers—a break.

They cannot be hit over the head with the same book month after month. So stop doing that. Cycle through your backlist, consistently and constantly bringing new people in, simply using different entry points to your brand and your catalog. It's much easier, much saner, and doubly successful, in my experience and opinion.

Remember how mileage varies per author? Same thing here. These are my opinions, based on my own experiences in the industry for the past 12 years. Through my author coaching, I can't tell you how many people message me on the verge of tears, because they're one breath away from burning out.

They publish 12 books a year. I publish 40, and I'm going strong.

I don't focus on EVERYTHING all at once, and I think that's the main difference between me and other authors.

Okay, I'm off the soap box. Let's look at October.

October 2018: $1529.34. I'm not worried. See above if you are. Let's gear up for two releases in the same month, AND a big Cyber Monday promo!

November 2018: The Brave Billionaire had a 73-day preorder at full price and came out on November 2. I did not discount it upon release. I let it come out. I sent it to my newsletter. I did not set up swaps, as by October I was not convinced of their effectiveness. (I'm still not, and do very little swapping.) I did not buy ads. I released the book, sent my newsletter, and set up some AMS ads. That was all.

Brave made: $1183.52

Series made: $3612.92

The Belated Billionaire had a 74-day preorder at full price and came out on November 19. I did the same thing for it that I did for Brave, which is to say, I released it at full price. I sent to my newsletter. I set up an AMS ad, and I enjoyed turkey for Thanksgiving.

The week following that—Cyber Monday! I set up a huge clean billionaire sale on the 8 books. The other co-author joined in. The whole series – up to 12 books now – was on sale for 99¢ on Kindle Countdown Deals (US and UK only).

We both sent to our newsletters. I had one swap set up with another author. I bought ads—My Book Cave, Read Cheaply, Love Kissed, and eBook Hounds. Those ads cost $140.

Belated made: $820.24

Series made: $3612.92

Some thoughts on this. You might have noticed that these last two books didn't make as much as the first six. They were Book 11 and 12 in the series, as there's a co-author who released 4 books in between.

Have readers not carried through her books? Unsure.

Do they just need more time to read her books? Probably.

I launched these new releases at $2.99, not 99¢. I did what I said NOT to do—I didn't start as I meant to go.

I started Elana with live launches at 99¢. But these last two books were preorders at $2.99, with no sale price upon launch.

I made less money.

Now, there could be other factors to this, as I was also launching a separate beach romance series, one book every 11 weeks, with long preorders at $3.99, and they do just fine. So what is it?

Does this specific niche not support full-price books? <<This lit a light bulb in my head, and I went in search of any sweet billionaires being launched at $2.99.

Couldn't find them.

So this is a case of being slightly off the market, and you know what? That's okay with me.

Shocking, I know!

But I simply don't want to launch every one of my books at 99¢. I think they have more value than that, and I'll probably have to claw my way up a hill to get the same readers as those 99¢-book authors.

But how I mean to go is to charge $2.99 or more for my work. So I have to do that, and do it consistently.

Just food for thought, here in November.

December 2018: $1946.71. At this point, I decide to lay off the series for a variety of reasons. I feel like I've brought in the people I'm going to bring in for now. There are still co-authors releasing books in the series, which should help me. All of my beach romances—Elana's brand—were falling, falling, falling.

Seasonal books?

I wasn't sure, as Elana is only 8 months old and has never lived through a winter as a beach romance author. But my ads were costing more, and I was seeing less ROI, and I turned them off for now.

I simply focused somewhere else, where I had better success. This is not failure. This is being a smart marketer and business manager, who looks at data to drive decisions.

And the data was telling me that perhaps the billionaire market was saturated. At least the people I was reaching had likely already bought the books. And it was time to do something different, at least for a season.

From May 1 – December 31, these 8 books earned me $40,672.81. That's more than I make in a year of teaching.

I was happy with them.

Something else to note:

I mentioned this above, but there are 15 books in this series. I've written 8 of them. I have two co-authors who write and publish in the series as well. Their releases should theoretically lift mine, though we're not dependent on each other for that. All the books are standalone novels, and we each publish them ourselves, with very little crossover. They're simply set in the same location.

That said, I think that by having control of the first 6 books, I have the most power to bring people into the entire series, and I've been working hard to do that.

I can't focus on every book or even every series each month. It's too expensive, and I'd never get any writing done.

I did a sale on these sweet beach billionaires in March, and another one on the boxed set in April, 2019, where it broke into the Top 100 on Amazon. And I'm done with them for a while. I've been pushing them and pushing them, and people now need that time we've talked about to get through my books, as well as the rest of the series.

So onward!

Recap:

1. What did you see here that you could try?
2. Ask yourself: Have I tried building a readership with live launching books at a very low price point? Why wouldn't I want to do this for me personally?
3. Can you write, edit, package, and release two books at the same time? Yikes! It was intense, I'm not going to lie.

4. In your mind, what advantages does this Rapid Release strategy have?
5. What did you think of my data on 99¢ releases? Have you found yours to be similar? Different? What do you think the difference is?

Notes and Things To Try:

15

RAPID RELEASING EVERY MONTH - CASE STUDY 6

This is the method I've settled on. I started doing this in October 2017, and by January 2018, I hit the USA Today bestseller list as a solo author with Book 4. After that, I started a strategy where I release two Liz Isaacson series each year.

Each series has 6 books in it.

One series runs from January – June. The next from July – December.

I've executed this strategy, releasing a new book every month in these core series, successfully for about 18 months at the time of writing.

I release more often than this, to be clear. I'm in collaborative projects and did a bunch of Kindle Worlds type of projects throughout 2017 and 2018. I've backed waaaaay off on those, as I find them to be my worst releases. The data tells me so, and since one of my goals is to make money, I'm going to use the strategies and practices that lead me toward that.

And author collaborations, shared worlds, and the like aren't really doing that for me. The numbers don't lie. You might find the complete opposite to be true. That's okay! We can still be friends. As always in Indie publishing, your mileage may vary. That's why I'm simply sharing what I've done and the fruits from it. Then you get to decide what you want to do with the ideas, strategies, and details provided.

So let's look specifically at the Christmas in Coral Canyon Romance series, which, technically, was 6 books over the course of 5 months. I was a month behind because of the USA Today bestselling book in January. So the data might be a bit skewed. I know I can see that, as Book 5 is my lowest earner. It only got a week to shine, and then Book 6 was out.

But I still think this series release sums up how I'm operating my business at the time of writing.

In this strategy, we see the Tiered Launch Strategy hard, hard at work. It's still something I'm doing as 2019 progresses, and I'm seeing really good results with it.

I have to operate like this, because my Liz Isaacson backlist is over 60 titles at the time of writing. And my Elana Johnson backlist is nearing 20. There simply is no way to advertise every single book that comes out.

I released 40 books in 2018. I have 50 on my schedule

for 2019. Yes, it's crazy. No, I wouldn't recommend it to anyone. But I learned how to do what I'm doing over the course of the past 12 years as I defined and redefined my writing chops, my personal writing philosophies, and found things that work for me, based on real numbers and data.

Will I be able to continue at this pace in 2020? Who knows? Even next month is up in the air! I've been working on implementing systems to sell my books over the course of the past 18 months, so even if I get sick or can't write for a while, I will still have income.

Systems are important. But this book isn't about systems, though everything I've outlined in these case studies are wide open windows into my systems. How I write. The schedules I use. The reasons for why I promote what book, and when. That's all a system.

Once you know what you can personally do, what you can afford, and what you're willing to risk, that system can keep you on-track. But you won't know until you try something. So don't be afraid to get out there and try!

Let's look at Christmas in Coral Canyon. Finally. Jeez.

August 9, 2018 - Book 1, Her Cowboy Billionaire Best Friend releases. This is a Tier 2 release. It's Medium. I sent it to my NL. I asked a friend to send to hers. I put up AMS ads on the book. Done.

NOTE: Almost **all** of my Book 1s are handled this

way. Medium release. Announce to NL. They've been on preorder for 90 days. Start AMS ads with tested and optimized lists. That's it. That's a Medium release in a nutshell.

The series earned $2781.44 in August. That's one book.

September 6, 2018 - Book 2, Her Cowboy Billionaire Boss releases. This is a Tier 1 release. It's a Hard push, Tier 1 release. I sent to my NL over the course of 5 days—so I segment out to spread sales out instead of getting a spike on release day.

I set up AMS ads with optimized lists AND start FB ads with a tested and tried audience. These have higher spends than Medium releases.

I price Book 1 at 99¢ on a Kindle Countdown Deal (if in Kindle Select). I buy 1-2 ads (like Robin Reads or Bargain Booksy or the like) for Book 1.

I push the sale on social media, in my NL, and through any other means (texting club, swaps, author takeovers).

NOTE: For this launch, I didn't have my texting crew yet. I didn't set up swaps. And I didn't do any author takeovers. I did everything else though.

THE GOAL: Get people into the new series who may have missed Book 1. Now they have 2 to read—and a third on preorder.

The series earned $6156.34 in September. 2 books.

. . .

October 4, 2018 - Book 3, Her Cowboy Billionaire Boyfriend releases. This is a Tier 3 Release. It's Soft. It's what I call a Sleeper. I do hardly anything with this release. Almost ALL of my Book 3s and Book 4s are sleepers. I send to my NL segmented over 3 days. I put up posts on social media. I start a low-level AMS ad and test an audience on FB with $10/day. I do this to have an audience to use later. If the first one doesn't work, I try another until I find one on FB that works well for THIS particular book. The series earned $7056.60 in October. 3 books.

November 8, 2018 - Book 4, Her Cowboy Billionaire Bodyguard releases. This is a Tier 3 Release. See above. The series earned $8103.78 in November. 4 books.

December 11, 2018 - Book 5, Her Cowboy Billionaire Bull Rider releases. This is a Tier 3 Release, because I'm gearing up for next week when I'm going to KILL THE SALES with the release of Book 6 in the series, on a hard-core Tier 1 release.

Sometimes I make Book 5 my hard-core Tier 1 release. Sometimes I don't. It all depends on what else is in the hopper. In this case, it was Book 6 and the retirement party that went with it.

So I didn't do much with this book but announce it because it came out on my birthday. I saved everything I had for....

December 18, 2018 - Book 6, Her Cowboy Billionaire Bachelor releases. This is a live launch. Not a preorder. And it launched at 99¢ instead of $3.99, like all the other books. This is a hard-core Tier 1 release.

Strategy:

Book 1 - free for all five KDP Select days. December 18 - 22.

Books 2 - 5 - 99c on Kindle Countdown Deals. You make twice as much on these. No, they're not world-wide, but as long as you tell your people that, it's very lucrative. December 18 - 20 ONLY. This is a limited-time, hurry-up-and-get-the-book sale.

Book 6 - 99c EVERYWHERE. December 18 - 20. Limited time sale. Get the whole series for less than five bucks. Three days only.

I booked about 50 NL swaps for this book, many of them solo placements, stacked over 3 days. I hit my list up front on Day 1.

I bought 3 ads for Book 1 at free, to hit one per day on the first 3 days of the sale, while the other books were 99¢.

On Day 4, the prices on the other books went up, and I started Facebook ads at high spend levels on Book 1, 2, 6, and the series as a whole (all six links in the ad copy, one for each book in the series).

And I sat back and watched. From December 22 - January 31—about 6 weeks—I made $46,479.30 on those 6 books. This does not include the money earned in August, September, October, or November. This is money ON TOP of that money. The series has earned just shy of $80,000 since going live on August 9, 2018.

You can make money on your books when YOU want to make money on them. I think that needs to be said again. **You can make money on your books when YOU want to make money on them.**

Now, everyone's asking, "Yes, great. But how much did you spend?" $8849.88 from December 18 - January 31. I'll spend $9000 to make $46,500 all day long. On just 6 books in my backlist. Work that's ALREADY been done. Because each of those books has links to other books of mine. More readers. More books getting read. Oh, and a Kindle All-Star Bonus earned.

Not every release is created equal, and it might be time for you to start thinking about a Tiered Release Strategy. It could save you time, mental energy, money, and more. It could help your backlist make money while you write the next book—which you'll strategically release.

If you'd like to see screenshots and download a blank

PDF for help planning your next Tiered Release, you can go to Liz Isaacson's website for that.

Recap:

1. What did you see here that you could try?
2. Ask yourself: Have I tried releasing books in a Tiered Launch Strategy? Why wouldn't I want to do this for me personally?
3. Can you write and release a book every month?
4. In your mind, what advantages does this Rapid Release strategy and this Launch strategy have?
5. What ad platforms and knowledge would you need to do this strategy? Are there courses or classes you can take to learn them? Do you have the money to spend in testing and on advertising? I teach a great Amazon Advertising course with my friend Bonnie Paulson. Search for Finding Your Indie on Teachable.
6. What can you do to grow your newsletter? My newsletter plays a pivotal role in my success, and I've been building it for 3.5 years. You can't expect to be in a similar place as me if you haven't had the time, money, or knowledge to do so. So be patient with yourself and your

process. Learn what works for you. Make adjustments as necessary. Be unafraid and unapologetic. This is a marathon, not a sprint.

Notes and Things To Try:

16

WRAPPING UP!

Holy mother of pearl. That was a lot, wasn't it? I know it was. But hopefully you bought the book, and you can come back to it anytime you want. Make notes. Make some more. Try a strategy and see how it works for you.

I think one of the points of this book, for me, was to show that it's a great time to be an Indie author. You can literally try anything you want. The experimentation is my absolute favorite part of being an Indie author.

I learned a lot of valuable lessons for each one of the Rapid Release strategies I've tried, and I hope you've learned something too!

One of the most important lessons I've learned is that you can easily overwhelm yourself and your readers when you start releasing too quickly. I learned this with Case

Study 2 and Case Study 3, releasing books in two series simultaneously.

The preorders went down. The sales went down. I was building my infrastructure, sure, but it wasn't large enough to accommodate so many books (12 of them in 9 months) at full price releases.

That was very valuable to me, and after that I started releasing once a month under Liz Isaacson, with the Summer 2018 Rapid Release being the only exception. She does really well at that pace, and at this point, there's no reason to increase it.

Elana is brand new in the sweet adult romance genre, and her strategies look a little bit different. That's totally okay. I actually think it's valuable to have different approaches, so you can look at the data for yourself and know what works for you and your books.

We've covered so much in this book! From setting Smart goals, to starting out the right way, to how to structure your writing time to write quickly, to all the different kinds of Rapid Release.

Along the way, I've talked about a lot of things, I know! Everything from distributors to Kindle Unlimited to price points to tracking software.

There is a lot out there to make an Indie author's life easier. There are a lot of people around to help. I hope you'll join me on Facebook on my Indie Inspiration page, where I post content at least three times a week for Indie authors in all stages of their careers.

Hopefully, you feel excited about the next stage of your career, and hopefully you've formed a strategy for your own Rapid Release writing or releasing.

Recap:
Do three things now:

1. Write down one goal you're going to set and work toward from reading this book.
2. Write down one writing strategy you're going to try to implement to write faster.
3. Write down one marketing strategy you want to try with your next release.

Good luck out there! And don't forget, you can find all the resources, PDFs, spreadsheets, and more on the Rapid Release resources page: http:// elanajohnson.com/resources

RESOURCES

You can find information about my ads courses, get the word tracking spreadsheet, as well as a list of my must-read books on marketing on my website: http://elanajohnson.com/resources

ABOUT ELANA

Elana Johnson is the USA Today bestselling author of dozens of clean and wholesome contemporary romance novels. She lives in Utah, where she mothers two fur babies, taxis her daughter to theater several times a week, and eats a lot of Ferrero Rocher while writing. Find her on her website at elanajohnson.com.